"An Empowered Life, written by a young man with a passion for God is very inspiring. If read on a daily basis will inspire you to face the challenges that you encounter on a daily basis. You will be empowered to rise above your situation and be propelled to fulfill your God-ordained assignment and ultimately reach your destiny."

—Elder Norman Nunes, Belfield Holiness Born Again

"This book will be an inspiration to others as they go through life with its varied trials and circumstances and seek to have a closer walk with him."

— Elder Ransford Stewart, Wiltshire Holiness Born Again

"These nuggets of encouragement and stories of strength will inspire the reader to walk in victory day by day and grow in the grace of God through a consistent relationship with the Lord."

— Pastor Odane James, Transformation Centre, Florida"

"This book is a must read. There is a word for every situation, every day and everyone. I truly wish we will apply these thoughts practically to our lives"

- Evangelist Simon McKenzie, Ducemain Apostolic

An Empowered Life

A Daily Dose of Inspirational Messages
for Self-Development and
Transformation

By

Eston Swaby

Eston Swaby

USA

Reason for this book

I love to encourage and motivate others; that is my heart's desire, to motivate and encourage people. I always tell my friends that I encourage and try to inspire people, because when I am going through my problems most times there is no one to give me a word to uplift my spirit; I therefore have to do as David did and encourage myself. Isn't it interesting that the ones who feed the spirits of others most times have no one to feed their spirits?

I strongly believe that it is a part of my ministry, or purpose in life, to play my part in imparting words of wisdom to all those who have ever questioned their purpose in life and even thought of suicide; those who have been bruised by other's words; those who have been belittled and looked down on by others; those who are wondering why they are facing all the things they are confronted with on a daily basis and need strength to overcome; those who feel out of place in society; those who feel like throwing in the towel; those who are involved in ministry, or have a gift, vision or dream and can't understand why they are confronted with so many opposing circumstances that seem to go against the promise of God; those to whom God has made promises and they are not seeing them being fulfilled in their lives and they are about to give up on that promise, and those who are struggling to go higher in God.

I have faced a lot of opposition and opposing circumstances in my short time being on earth, so that sometimes I question if God loves me. Many times I tried to give up on God and throw in the towel, saying, "God, I will never serve you again", "Lord, you have deceived me, I am finished with serving you", but like Jeremiah I could not throw in the towel because God is not finished with me as yet, and neither is he finished with you! God wants me to tell you that you are uncontainable, and he wants to take you to another level in ministry, your career and in other aspects of your life...

For feedback, interviews or any other engagements, please get in touch with me at:

www.estonswaby.com

Also on Social Media

Twitter: @estonswaby   Facebook: estonswabypage

Acknowledgement

I would like to take a moment to express my gratitude to some people who have extended their wisdom, knowledge and gave a listening ear. Firstly I would like to say thanks to all the people who have cheered me on during the writing and publishing process; Rueben Johnson for reading through my manuscript and pointing out errors; my editor Rachel Fogg for editing my manuscript; Elder Ransford Stewart for his words of encouragements and time, and all the other people that have contributed to this book in some way.

You all have contributed to this book, and I am very grateful for the parts you all have played in making this book possible. For all those I failed to mention, please accept my gratitude for your support. I also want to thank YOU, the reader for buying my book. Without you the reader, this project could not be a success.

And of course, this book would not have been possible without the inspiration, ability and strength God has given me; without him I would be nothing.

Part 1

Facing Life Struggles

Day 1
A God of Strategies

"God is a God of strategies. There are times we may think that our life is going in the wrong direction, but it's all a part of God's divine will for you. Like Joseph was strategically sent into Egypt as a slave, so the Lord uses obstacles to strategically position us in the place he wants us."

Scriptures of the Day: Genesis 39: 1-23; 45:1–11

Discourse

Like Joseph, there are many of us who God has given a dream. God says he will make you a ruler and not a slave, but everything happening in your life is going contrary to what God said. God said he will bless you financially, but all you are seeing is unpaid bills and no money to get you through the rest of the month.

If you are one of the millions of people in this position, then this message is for you.

God sometimes will strategically lead us down a path that may seem like we are going in the wrong direction, but God knows what he is doing. God know where he wants you to be ten years from now, and just how to get you there. He knows that if he does not at times allow you to face some stormy seas, setbacks, betrayals and so on, you will not have what it takes to be who he called you to be. His ways do not always seem straight or fair, but his will is sovereign and he knows what he is doing. He is not a God who wakes up one morning and decides to send trouble your way; neither is he a God that can be taken by surprise by your trials, or a God whose purpose in your life can be abandoned. At times he may allow us to take a detour, but his purpose for you will always be fulfilled. If he said it, then it shall come to pass. God showed Joseph when he was 17 years of age that he would be a ruler, but he did not tell or show Joseph the path to the throne. God will show us our purpose and where he is taking us- he is going to make you the CEO of your company, you're going to own your own business, you're going to travel the world preaching the gospel, He is going to make you a pastor- but he will not show you the pit in between the spoken Word or vision and the fulfillment of the promise. Jesus did not tell his disciples that on their way across the lake to go to the other side they would encounter a storm that would threaten to kill them. Why? Because he wanted them to trust him that whatever may come between the spoken Word or promise and the fulfillment of that Word or promise, he would take them through it and bring them to where he said he would take them.

Sometimes if God would show us the path we will have to take to our ministry, purpose or blessing, we would back out and say, 'No, Lord, its okay, I'll pass.' The thoughts God has towards you are of peace and to give you an expected end - not to destroy you.

For the promise to be fulfilled in Joseph's life, he had to be hated by his brothers, thrown in a pit and then sold as a slave in Egypt- the country he would be made ruler of. The pit is not there to keep you down, it is there to elevate you to greatness, because the way up is always down. Do not worry about those who looked down on you and stepped on you, as they are just a stepping stone to where God wants to take you. God knew that in order for you to be great, He first had to allow people to hate you, look down on you, step on you, and so on. He knew that you would not give up, but would use what you have been through to take you higher. However, sometimes we allow what God sends to make us strong and to strategically place us in our purpose to deter us from the path. It's like when walking on a pathway to somewhere, there sometimes will be obstacles on that path, but if we allow these obstacles to stop us then we will not reach the end of the pathway. Joseph was in Egypt as a slave, but slavery was God positioning him for his purpose. God may have told you that you will be the head of a company, but sometimes to make you the head, He first has to allow you to take a job as the Janitor of the company he wants you to manage.

Everything that happened to Joseph was in God's plan: hated by his brothers, thrown in the pit, sold in slavery, Potiphar's wife lied about him and he was thrown in prison for a crime he did not commit, the promise by Pharaoh's butler to put in a good word to the king for him that the butler forgot. Years of betrayal, imprisonment, disappointments, and rejection were to take Joseph to the throne. Everything seemed like it was going in the wrong direction, but it was all a part of the process and everything happened in God's time, not his. Even though Joseph could not see what God was doing, he kept his eyes on God.

Moving Forward

As you go through this day, what is happening in your life that seems contrary to your vision, or the promise of God? Maybe you are feeling forsaken by God, or like God has forgotten about his promises, but He hasn't. What you are going through is all a part of God's design for your life. I know, because I have been right where you are now. We all want God to take us into our purpose, but first before we can go up we must first go down into our valley. What God is asking of you is that you do not stop on one of those stones, as it's not where God wants you to be; the stepping stone is a stone put in your path for you to reach where God wants you to be. The valley you find yourself in is to take you to the other side of the mountain, a higher mountain than the one you are coming from. Joseph was in the pit, but the pit was not his final destination; it was just the foundation for his elevation.

You may be in your pit right now, but don't lose focus and don't lay in self-pity, as where you are now is not your final destination; you haven't seen all you are fully capable of as yet. Will you trust Him when your life is taking a U-turn? Will you trust Him when you don't understand? God does not expect you to stop in the wilderness, but He expects you to continue into the promise land. God bless you.

Day 2
Built to Handle Life's Challenges

"Like a building is constructed to handle a certain amount of pressure, so God has built each one of us to handle the level of test and temptations we may face."

Scriptures of the Day: 1 Corinthians 10: 13; Ephesians 1: 13-14; 4:7-13; James 1:12

Discourse

Have you ever looked at a bridge, or even the chair you may be sitting on right now, and wondered how is it able to handle the amount of pressure that is thrown at it on a daily basis? For example, many bridges have to hold the pressure of very heavy duty trucks that pass by several times a day. How is it possible to manage the constant pressure of heavy duty vehicles? How is it that the bed or seat you're on now is able to handle the pressure you put on it on a daily basis?

This is because everything in life is designed to handle a certain level of pressure. When architects and designers are constructing buildings and other things that will be used by us, they first consider the expected weight it will have to carry before they design it and make it available.

Why am I saying all this to you? I want to tell you that before God allowed you to be placed in certain situations, He first constructed you to handle the pressure. Yes, you will feel the heat of the pressure, and sometimes we will have to ask for help; but God will never allow you to be tested more than you are able to bear. The Bible says,

"There hath no temptation taken you but such as is common to man: but God is faithful, who will not suffer you to be tempted above that ye are able; but will with the temptation also make a way to escape, that ye may be able to bear it"- 1 Corinthians 10:13.

That is because God first had to ensure that you are able to handle the level of temptation and test before He allowed the enemy to test and or tempt you. God said unto Satan one day, 'Have you considered my servant, Job?' God was able to boast about Job because He knew that Job had enough experience and strength to deal with any attacks the enemy may throw at him. In response, the enemy let God know that the reason God is able to boast about Job is because God had put a fence of protection around Job; I want to tell you that Satan cannot test you with suffering, affliction, persecution and everything life throws in your face without God allowing it or giving him permission to do so. This means that God chooses what we face and at what level. This tells us that:

1. Everything we face has a purpose- whether it may be to prove to Satan or those around us that God is who He says He is, or it may be one of many reasons, or it is for any divine purpose.

2. God has given you the strength to overcome your pain, suffering, affliction, infirmities and life struggles. God said unto Paul, "My grace is sufficient for thee: for my strength is made perfect in weakness"- 2 Corinthians 12:9. When you are weak, God shows up strong.

Moving Forward

As you go through this day and face all that life has to throw at you, remember you were built to stand. God hand-picked and designed you in such a manner that the enemy is afraid of you. He is afraid that if you realize who you really are, then all that he is doing is futile. Always remember this: How you think about your trials will be the deciding factor if you come out as a victor or a victim. Which one will you be?

Day 3
Having Persistent Faith

"What do you do when God says no? Many people will have you to think that if you have enough faith God will always say yes to you. Your faith will save your mom from death, will heal you of cancer when you ask. But what do you do when you have enough faith but God still says no?"

Scriptures of the Day: Mark 14: 32-36; 2 Corinthians 12:7-10

Discourse

If you are one of those people who think that if you have enough faith then you will always get what you want, then you are not alone - I too was one who thought that if I had enough faith, God would have let me get that job I wanted (I actually started making plans and telling friends that I was getting a new job - I just got called for an interview - because I had faith), if I had enough faith I would have completed my education according to my plan, I would have had my dream house right now and the list goes on. I don't know anyone who is as powerful as my pastor, who God has used to bring healing to many people that have eye problems so they are no longer in need of eye glasses, but yet he had to get glasses because he has a hard time seeing, and his wife almost went blind; still they have great faith. I would like to tell you that even if you have faith that could move mountains, or you are as powerful as Elijah, God will not always say yes.

Many people would want you to believe that the reason you didn't get that job, or your child died, or you are not able to get pregnant, or your life seems to be going off track, or you are still sick, is because you do not have enough faith - your faith is weak. Because of this, many of us walk around feeling depressed because no matter what we do, we still do not have enough faith to move God to work on our behalf. You believed and told everyone you were getting that job, your mom would come out of the hospital, your child wouldn't die because God was on the job, you are getting better as God is going to make you walk again; but God said no. You and the whole church prayed and fasted, but God still said no.

What if he was the one who put you, or allowed you to be, in that situation in the first place?

We are told of a personal experience in the Bible with one of the greatest writers and apostles of all time, the apostle Paul. Paul was one of the greatest apostles in the Bible, who received an abundance of revelation, laid his hand and prayed and raised the dead, healed the sick, preached the gospel in many cities and turned many powerful cities upside down, who was feared by many and respected by others. He was a very powerful man of God, full of faith; but he had a very depressive issue. He had an infirmity of the flesh, a thorn in his flesh to buffet him lest he should be exalted above measure. For this he sought the Lord, not once or twice, but three times. This was a big thing for Paul to handle and so he said 'No, I cannot handle this thing any longer.' So he, with all his faith and all the credentials behind his name, preached the gospel to those in need, raised the dead, healed the sick, preached even while he was in prison, went where he was sent, and was so gifted and special that he was taken up into the third heaven. He did not go to God about being shipwrecked, he did not go to God about getting out of prison, he didn't go to God and beg God to reduce his persecution, affliction and sufferings. He did not go to God and ask him to stop letting people hate and want to destroy him. He did not go to God for riches to do his work and to live a happy life. But...he went to God asking God to remove this thorn in his flesh, "For this thing I besought the Lord thrice, that it might depart from me" (2 Corinthians 12:8). He asked God for a small thing and God said NO. The one time he had a problem and needed it dealt with God said no, request denied. 'But God, I didn't come to you asking you to get me out of prison...' No, request denied. 'But God, I didn't complain or beg you not to let me get shipwrecked...' No, request denied. The man who did so much for God, and had such great faith that he could raise the dead, did not have his request granted. He saw the power of God every day, the sick being healed, dead raised, signs and wonders through his ministry, he gave up his high-class life and friends to serve God, but this one thing he asked God for, he did not get. Jesus was the closest to the Father and yet after asking for his life three times had to say in the end, Lord let your will be done.

What do you do when God says no to an embarrassing issue you've been having, when he allows your only child to die, when you have been doing everything you can for him and serving him with all your heart, but he does not allow you to get that job you wanted, when sickness is rocking your body and he says you have to go through it?

God said to Paul, Paul I know you have done so much in serving me and you have been faithful in preaching my word, the reason why I didn't grant you your request and remove this issue is because, "My grace is sufficient for thee: for my strength is made perfect in weakness" (2 Corinthians 12:9). 'Paul, you're troubled with this right now, but you will have to endure it because your issue shows how strong I am.'

I want to tell someone reading this book right now that God cares very much about you. It is not because he wants you to suffer or go through the stuff you're currently going through, but he wants you to know that before he puts you in a certain situation, he measures what you are able to bear with the strength he is giving you to go through it. He says as thy day is, so is thy strength (Deuteronomy 33:25); what that means is the bigger the situation is, the bigger the strength he has given you to endure it. Yes, you may be depressed right now; yes, your co-workers and boss are making every day at work very difficult for you; yes, sickness may be rocking your body right now; yes, the person He blessed you with is about to die; yes, you are about to lose your home and everything you have worked hard for; yes, your marriage is in turmoil; yes, your back is against the wall right now and you don't know where to turn- but God is saying to you right now that He has given you the strength to endure it and come out as pure gold. You may not think you can handle this thing you're going through and it's too much for you to bear, but "as thy days, so is thy strength be." God will never give you more than you are able to bear. His grace is enough to take you through your problems. I will not tell you that your situation will get any better soon, I will not tell you you're going to understand right now why you're facing certain situations in your life, but I want you to trust God. You may say, 'God, this is too much for me to bear.' God would not ask you to trust Him if it wasn't important.

David sought the Lord for his son in fasting and prayer for many days, but his son still died (2 Samuel 12:15-24). When his son died he got up, ate and worshipped the Lord. Why? It was not because he didn't love and want the child to live, but he rose up ate and worshipped because he realized that God had given him the grace to endure the pain of losing a child; God said no, no, your child will die. Of course it took him a while to get over the death of his child, but God was his comforter. You may cry yourself to sleep, walk with your head down, or feel depressed; you might have to endure poverty, hunger, or not having good clothes to wear, but God loves you and wants you to know that he sees your situation, but in his divine will he knows he has given you the strength to go through it. Not only that, you will have a shout in the end.

Moving Forward

As you go through this day with this issue over your head, and as you face the rest of your life, I want you to know that God will not always say yes to you, no matter who you are, how much faith you have or how gifted you are. God, in his sovereignty, at times will choose to deny our request. He denies it at times because God has entrusted you with trouble, and sometimes he gives us a thorn to buffet us so we will not become high-minded. I want to encourage you to hold on to God and not lose faith in his love for you. You may cry now, but I promise you if you endure the pain of being rejected you will have your shout. I want to tell you that the sickness or issue you're now facing will not destroy you, but that God will use it for his glory. What do you do when God says no? You trust and wait upon him.

Day 4
Your Value Never Changes

"Broken, but in the right places. In life, regardless of what people may do and say to you, no matter what life hurdles you have to face, your value does not change."

Scriptures of the Day: Genesis 1: 26-28; Psalms 139:13-16; Ephesians 2:4-9

Discourse

What if I should give you $500US right now, would you want it? What if I should crush it; would you still want it? What if I should step on it; would you still want it? I am sure you would. Why? Because no matter what I do to it or how old it is, its value never changes.

Many of us were crushed beyond measure by significant others such as our parents, intimate partners, friends, people whom we associate with, and co-workers, among others. We are made to feel less than who God says we are, while some of us have lost our identity and purpose in life because of others. Many of us are fearful of stepping out or doing things, because we have been crushed so many times in the past that we are intimidated by others.

I wrote this book to let you know if you are one of the millions of people who are crushed by life, I want to tell you that God sees everything. He may not have intervened when you were laughed at, belittled, humiliated, cast down and walked all over, or when your father or mother hit you until you felt like you were going to die, but he saw it and he wants you to know you were broken, but in the right places; broken, but not according to the will of Satan. Life crushed you, but he wants you to use your pain, all that you have been through, all those negative words people used at you on a regular basis; he wants you to use all that you have been through and are going through to help others.

You may feel like you are not important or valuable, but you are valuable to God. Jesus died so that you may know your value. You have so much value that the enemy is afraid of you and wants to take away what God has invested in you before it can be manifested.

Just like how the crushed and dirty $500US bill doesn't loses its value, likewise, no matter what happens to you in life, your value doesn't change. In fact, your experiences have made you a lot more valuable than you were. You may ask, how so? Well, let me tell you: for most of my life I was crushed by the words of others; by the words of my father so much that before he gave his life to God most times I was afraid to be in his presence; crushed by the words of my co-workers at times; crushed by people who boasted and looked down on me because of my weakness and my inability at times to purchase certain things; crushed by my mistakes. Many times I would look at others and compare myself to them, oftentimes wishing I was them; many times I wished I was never born or that God would take my life. I hated my life, and secretly was mad at God for all he allowed me to go through, not to mention doubted his love for me. Why should he when I didn't love myself? Like the apostle Paul rejoiced in his persecution and afflictions, so now I rejoice in all I have been through. Why? I have learnt that I am now more valuable because of all I have been through. My experiences have led me to write this book you're reading now; my experiences have put me in a position where I am able to minister to many who felt like giving up, many who were troubled by things that pushed them over the edge. How many people have I ministered to or counseled who wanted to give up on life, but are now living and serving God because God trusted me with my pain and afflictions?

Moving Forward

As you go through this day and face the rest of your life, I want you to understand that your experiences have made you more valuable than you were before those experiences. Thousands of international and motivational speakers travel the world, encouraging and ministering to millions, because life crushed them and they have overcome. They were broken, but in the right places. Who is waiting on your testimony? Some of you reading this book right now need to start writing a book about all you have been through; if you write it, I am sure someone will read it.

Day 5
Your Problems Serve a Purpose

"Your problems serve a purpose. The reason why you're going through some of the things you are facing now is because the enemy knows that God has invested something great in you that is a great threat to his kingdom. Let us not focus on the troubles we go through, but embrace our pain, as God is using our pain to prepare us to complete a great work. Your pain is a part of the process that will bring out what's in you."

Scripture of the Day: Genesis 45:1–11

Discourse

How close do you want to be to God? Where do you want to reach in life? Whatever you need to be, who God has created you to be, he has already given it to you, or you are in the process of having it; in fact, it was invested in you before you were even born, and only starts to manifest in its season. For example, your intellect, your mind, your handicap (yes, your handicap serves a purpose), your strength, your struggles, your past experiences and the list goes on. You may think that God cannot use these things to fulfill his purpose in your life, but he can. God let the jackass die and his bone to be ready when Samson was in a battle so Samson could use that jackass' bone to defeat his enemies (Judges 15:15). What you need to make your life better, to impact your generation, to change the world, to change the destiny of your family, God has already given it you; it's just for you to reach and grab it.

You may ask, 'What do I have that the Lord will use to bring glory to his name or use to make a difference in the lives of others?' The simple answer is, your problems! All the things you have been through, or currently facing, and will face until the day you die. Your problems serve a purpose.

You may look at yourself and say my problem is that I am small in stature, or my problem is that I come from a very poor family and live in one of the worst communities in my country, or I didn't graduate from high school, or I have low self-esteem, people treat me as a nobody, and the list goes on. But do you know you can use your handicap, your background, how others see you, your status in life, and your weakness and change the world? Dr. Cindy Trimms grew up in poverty and now she is impacting the world through her business, books and her teachings. Many motivational speakers suffer from many handicaps not to mention the fact that many life changing books were written by people who were marginalized by society and others around them. Naaman, in the Bible, who God used to defeat the Israelites, was a leper; by all customs he should be an outcast, a no-body. But he was the captain of the Syrian army and when he spoke, soldiers obeyed, and even the king held him in high regards; but he had a serious problem that should, and could destroy him- his leprosy (2 Kings 5:1-19).

Many times we ask God to use us and to order our steps in his will, but what if God has to first put you in the bed of affliction and pain before he can use you? What if the way he wants to use and or bless you is that he first has to allow you to be thrown in prison for a crime you didn't commit (like Joseph)? What if he first has to give you a near death experience so that you can testify before thousands of people, telling them of the saving power of God? What if for how he wants to use you, he first has to put you through poverty, and strip you of your job, family, home, bank account, and the list goes on? Would you still want him to use you? Would you still want him to order your steps? Would you still sing the song, 'Lord I am available to you, for you to use me as YOU please'? Is he only your God when things are going right, or will he still be your God when there is no food in the house and money in your pocket for an extended period of time? The way up is always down.

Jesus is the King of kings, and yet he was born and grew up in poverty, born in a manger and had to run for his life at a tender age. To add to all that, he grew up in what we would call today an inner-city community filled with criminals, and a place where it was expected that no good person would ever come out of (Nazareth); then he had to live his life treated as a madman and hated by many, before being charged with treason and dying on the cross like a criminal. All that Jesus went through taught us humility, endurance and helps us to go through our daily struggles, afflictions and persecutions.

God used Naaman to bring the Jehovah God that was in Israel to the Syrians, who were idol worshippers. To do that he had to make someone who they respected and held in high regard so sick that he had to go down to Israel, a nation which he conquered and caused the death of hundreds in, if not thousands. When Naaman dipped in the water the seventh time, he decided that he had to serve the God that brought him such great deliverance and so he offered sacrifices in Syria to the God of Israel. The sooner you stop looking at your problems as elephants in your life and start looking at them as instruments God is using to mold you into a vessel of honor, to bring you into your purpose, to save souls for his kingdom, and to affect your generation and even generations to come, the sooner you will start giving God glory and start thanking him for the struggles and pains, and start asking him, "Lord, what will you have me to do?"

They are people that you have talked to, worked with, and probably shared the word of God with that will never serve the God you worship, but God will use your deliverance, your problems, to convince them that there is a God who delivers, and there is a God of their situation. It doesn't matter who you are and what your problem may be, your problem serves a purpose; when life throws you a lemon, use it to make lemonade.

Moving Forward

If you don't get anything from this book and all the previous messages, I want you to understand that, YOUR PROBLEMS SERVE A PURPOSE and God wants to use your circumstances to either: elevate and bless you, put you in a position to help, inspire/motivate or bless others, humble you and teach you something, or your problems are there so that God may prove his awesome power and love through you and in you. God used Naaman's leprosy to humble and teach him that the God of Israel is a deliverer.

Your problems serve a purpose. What purpose does the Lord have for your life?

Day 6
Where is Your Focus?

"Whenever we start focusing only on what the enemy is doing, we start losing focus and sight of what God is doing."

Scriptures of the Day: Job 1:1-22; 23: 10

Discourse

Many times when we face situations in our life it is very easy, and always the first thing a person normally does, to focus on the problems, not the problem solver (God). As soon as problems come our way and the enemy is attacking every aspect of our lives we begin to start complaining, asking God what you did wrong or to take you out of it, crying, running all over the place seeking help- and not stopping to ask the question, "Lord, you allowed this situation to come into my life, what is it that you're doing or teaching me through this situation?" God will use your problems to shape your life, teach you or someone else something, bring you into your ministry, or change how you think or behave.

Many times the Lord is about to do something in our life or take us somewhere we have never been, but the devil sees this; in order to hinder the move of God, he uses many distractions to get our focus elsewhere from where God wants to take us or what he wants to show us. Despite what the enemy is doing, if we can just look beyond our situation(s), then we will see God working behind the scene. Life is not always what it seems. Perhaps the enemy is showing you that you will always be in poverty and your children will never come to anything good in life, but I would like to encourage you to look past that and see God in every situation and start praising him for what he can and will do for you.

Additionally, many times the Lord will allow the enemy to attack us so as to prove to him that no matter what comes our way, we will be faithful to him. The Bible tells us of an upright and blameless man by the name of Job who God presented to Satan. Satan challenged God that if he should remove the hedge of protection from around Job, his family and all he has, then Job would curse God. This was when all hell, as Jamaicans would say, broke loose in his life to the point that Job lost everything, including his children. Job could not understand why all these calamities were happening in his life; but regardless of what he was facing, he never lost his integrity or charged God foolishly. God was using Satan to not only prove the faithfulness of Job, but also to set Job up for a greater blessing. Could this be what God is doing in your life?

Moving Forward

As you go through this day and face the rest of your life, remember no matter what your situation may be and how life looks now, God is on the job and he will come through for you. The reason why you are going through your circumstances now is because God trusts you with trouble, and therefore knows you can handle it. Look at how big God is, not at how big the situation is.

Job did not get distracted by what he was going through because he knew the God in whom he put his trust in; don't get distracted by all you face.

Day 7
God Has Not Forsaken You

"'Lord thou hast deceived me'; how many times have we said that to God? How many times have we told God that he did not keep his end of the bargain? Unfulfilled promises, ministry setbacks, life going off track, financial problems when God said your blessing is on the way two years ago, and the list goes on. At times we may think that God has forsaken us or has gone back on His promises, but His promise is sure. The promise(s) He gave you is for an appointed time. It will come; wait PATIENTLY for it by faith."

Scriptures of the Day: Jeremiah 1:1-10, 17-19; 20: 7-10

Discourse

Many of us can relate to the message above; God said He would give you something when you were 20 years old, and you're now 30 and God still hasn't done what He said He would do. It is at these times our spiritual umbilical cord, which is our faith, starts to loosen its hold to our source, which is God.

I will share with you two experiences:

1. I remember when the Lord called me to ministry or spoke over my life that I would teach His word I was very excited about this, as I love to study the Word of God. I had high hopes and thought that I would be well received when the Lord started to use me to teach His Word, but the opposite happened. Many people in positions did not want to hear me, I heard harsh words spoken against me, and even leaders said things and did things that I found hurtful; harsh words were even spoken about me in my presence, amongst other things. I wanted to quit and run, but I couldn't. I felt like Jeremiah, who cried unto the Lord, saying, "O LORD, thou hast deceived me, and I was deceived: thou art stronger than I, and hast prevailed: I am in derision daily, every one

mocketh me. For since I spake, I cried out, I cried violence and spoil; because the word of the LORD was made a reproach unto me, and a derision, daily. Then I said, I will not make mention of him, nor speak any more in his name. But his word was in mine heart as a burning fire shut up in my bones, and I was weary with forbearing, and I could not stay"- Jeremiah 20:7-9.

I told God the same thing Jeremiah told God, and literally told Him, I AM DONE! I didn't want to go back to church, and I started going later than I did before. It went so far that I did not want to read the Bible anymore, as whenever I read the Bible He would give me new revelations; I wanted nothing to do with the Word of God or teaching in that church again. However, like Jeremiah at the end of the day, even when I did not want to, all I wanted to do was study and teach the Word of God; it's in my DNA. I thought the Lord had deceived me, as His words were very inspiring and at first I wanted to run to teach, but after a while I wanted to pack my bag and run, just like many of you right now.

No one knows the pain you have to endure just to wake up in the morning, or the costs of doing the work of the Lord. No one knows what you give up just to do what the Lord calls you to do, and if you make a mistake, 'dog eat you for supper', as Jamaicans would say. No one knows, but everyone talks. The cost of ministry is very high.

2. Secondly, I remember the Lord made me a promise of blessings, and months after I saw nothing. People were being blessed, and I saw none of His promises. I gave up, for a short time. 'Lord, thou hast deceived me, again."

The Lord's timing is not our timing, and everything we go through is to make us stronger. The Lord will show us the house, but not the 10 years of waiting and what it will cost you to have that house; He will show us our ministry, but not the sleepless nights, persecution and oppositions we will have to face; He will show us our spouse and happy marriage, but not what it will take to have and keep your marriage intact. Jesus' family wanted to stop his ministry because they thought he was out of his mind (Mark 3:21).

What do you do when you know the Lord has called you to ministry but all hell is breaking lose in your life and ministry? When you cry yourself to sleep because of the slandering of those around you? What do you do when He calls you for a certain career path, but everything is working against you? What do you do when you're about to lose hope of His promises coming to pass and all you're thinking is, "O LORD, thou hast deceived me, and I was deceived"?

1. You rely on the Word of God, even when everything around you is not going as promised. Your faith will be tested, but He will often remind you of His promises and things He brought you through.

Every time I felt discouraged by the things I faced and the negative words of those around me, I would remember the promise of God, that He will highly exalt me and my ministry will take me very far.

2. You surround yourself with positive people who will remind you of what God said, not what is happening around you. I have s few friends around me that I call 'builders'. At times I feel discouraged and like I'm not important, and immediately they, without knowing how I am feeling, give me an uplifting word.

Moving Forward

As you go through this day, let us not lose sight of the promises of God, as He is faithful and He cannot and will never lie. If God said you will be a Professor, a manager of your own company, a Pastor or will have your own ministry, then it shall come to pass. Once you keep your end of the bargain, none of His promises will fail.

Day 8
Obstacles or Opportunities?

Stop seeing your obstacles as big elephants in a small room, but see them instead as opportunities God allows to come your way to help you grow, reinvent your methods, or for you to seek Him more.

Scriptures of the Day: 2 Timothy 2:15-22; Jeremiah 18:1-6

Discourse

There are three main purposes of obstacles that come in our life:

1. Our obstacles come to help us to grow to become who God wants us to be. All of us are like clay, and God is the potter. Like the potter molds the clay, so does the Lord mold us so that we may be vessels in the master's hands. Sometimes in making the vessels, the potter has to apply force or pressure to the clay so that he can pattern the clay into what is in the mind of the potter; likewise, God allows the pressures of life, for example, persecution, sickness, neighbors giving us problems, children etc., and not only does He allow these obstacles, but He chooses what obstacles we may face. This therefore means that everything that we may face is orchestrated by God for a powerful purpose- the devil throws the darts at us, but God turns it around for our good. That is why the Bible says that with every temptation or test, God will make a way of escape (1 Corinthians 10:13), as just like an engineer builds a bridge to withstand certain levels of pressure, so did the Lord build us that we may withstand what the enemy throws at us.

2. Our obstacles at times come to cause us to reinvent our methods, or to reposition ourselves. During our seasons of testing, at times God may be repositioning us for a greater purpose that we may not see at the

time, because we are focusing on what we lost and not seeing what God is doing or about to give us. Elijah received new direction for his ministry when he was at the lowest end of his life and had to run for his life. When the pressures of his ministry were getting to be too much, Elijah sat under a tree and prayed for death. It was then that the Lord visited him and told him to anoint Elisha to take his place, and to anoint a new king who would bring Jezebel's reign to an end (1 Kings 19).

The apostles and the early church, after Jesus gave them the commandment to preach the gospel throughout the world, became complacent at Jerusalem, so the Lord allowed persecution to uproot the church from its comfort zone; and thus the gospel spread to other parts of the world. Like the early church, there are times we may become complacent in our job, family life, ministry or our lives in general, when God wants us to go to another level; therefore, at times, He will cause obstacles or challenges to come into our lives so that He may reposition us for something greater.

3. The Lord will use obstacles to cause us to seek him more. Many of us can testify that the time we pray and seek the Lord most is when life challenges us; for example, when there is no food in the house, when we are without a job, when the kids or our spouse are giving us problems, when sickness is rocking our bodies, and the list goes on; that's the time we go down on our knees and pray to God often, or begin to fast. The Lord therefore will at times allow seasons of testing to draw us closer to Him.

The obstacles we face on a daily basis are not to destroy or to suffocate us, but they are to make us better. It is the enemy's job to let us see our obstacles as elephants in a small room, taking up needed space while suffocating us. It is the will of God that each one of us will use the obstacles we face to know Him more and grow to our full potential, as there is greatness in each one of us.

Each one of us is a secret weapon that the Lord is molding and setting up to do a mighty work on the earth. Like Esther who had to be purified for 12 months before she could stand before the king, and then became Queen of an empire, so does the Lord take us through a process so we can be fit for the master's use. God's plan for your life is not to destroy or to degrade you, but His thoughts toward you are to exalt you. He wants to put you in the palace, but before He can do that He must remove some people out of the way, and He must take you through a process. Every good and durable thing has to go through a process.

Additionally, sometimes God will put us in a wilderness situation to flex His muscles in our life, build our faith, take us to another level, glorify His name, etc. When this happens, don't murmur, but remember how the Lord brought you out of your last experience. Stand and see God work. Face your situation head on, as your victory is before you. The Egyptians (your obstacles) you see today, you'll see them no problem.

Moving Forward

As you go through this day, please consider that as a father chastises his son, so does the Lord use obstacles to chastise us so that we may be who He wants us to be. You may feel like giving up now because of the level of testing you are going through, but the Lord will give you the strength to overcome. His grace is sufficient to keep you.

Day 9
Overcoming Life Obstacles

"Obstacles are like a football/soccer match where opponents will try to block your shot at goal; that's their job, so every move you make is therefore precious and will determine the outcome of the match."

Scriptures of the Day: Hebrews 12:1-4, 11-13; Acts 4: 1-21

Discourse

Most of us have either watched or listened to at least one football/soccer match, either through the media, or we went to a football/soccer match. In a football/soccer match there are two teams playing against each other, both trying to outperform and outsmart each other with the aim of winning the game. It is a game in which each team is trying to score a goal against the other team, while the opponent team is trying to block or prevent the other team from scoring.

The obstacles we face each day in our lives can be likened to a football or soccer game, where each one of us is trying to accomplish or reach a desired level in our personal growth and or ministry; however, as we push towards achieving that desired objective, we face obstacles that come to hinder or stop us from reaching our destination. These obstacles may try to block or prevent us at work, in our family life, in our educational pursuits, or in our ministry.

However, despite all that we may face each day, the good thing is that everything we need to walk in our purpose, God has already given to us; the obstacle is to bring them out. We have the tools or keys to be who God wants us to be; for example, leadership skills that are in some of us waiting to be released, our talents, our intellect, and our skills, among others. The problem is that whenever the enemy sees that we are about to walk to or go towards fulfilling our destiny or purpose, he sends obstacles to stop us. He will send distractions such as illnesses, a spouse giving us problems, troubles at work, life crisis, the opposite sex, financial distress (and the list goes on) with the intention of either slowing us down, throwing us off track or destroying us totally.

Furthermore, he will send the spirit of Herod to kill the promised seed-our purpose; or, if that doesn't work, he will send the spirit of Jezebel to control you, undermine your purpose or intellect, to seduce and or to outright kill you.

There are two main truths I would like to share with you:

Truth #1- That is their purpose. The obstacles you may face come to stop and or hinder you from walking in your purpose; that's their job. Your job is to use everything God has given you to score that winning goal while preventing the enemy from doing likewise.

Truth #2- The fact that the enemy will send obstacles or opponents to stop you is a good thing. The reason why Elijah and Jehu were on the scene was because there was a Jezebel who needed to be stopped; Jezebel's presence showed Israel that Baal was not the true God when Elijah called down fire on the sacrifice at Mount Carmel. The power of God and your purpose are made more profound in your life when it seems like all hell is breaking loose in your life, and the enemy has sent out his best assassins to destroy you. The fact that he did proves your worth in the kingdom of God, and how much a threat you are to his (Satan's) kingdom. Whatever you carry, the devil is afraid of it. God says, "My grace is sufficient for thee: for my strength is made perfect in weakness" (2 Corinthians 12:9). The more He fights, the more you go down on your knees and pray to God, and the more the Lord proves Himself to you. So let the obstacles come. Let the heartaches, persecution and afflictions come, because the more the devil attacks, the more power you stand to receive and the more powerful your testimonies will be.

The Bible says, "And we know that all things work together for good to them that love God, to them who are the called according to his purpose...Nay, in all these things we are more than conquerors through him that loved us (Romans 8:28, 37)

These things represent your neighbors telling lies about you, your co-workers working together to destroy you, your spouse and or family attacking you, not being able to pay your bills, losing your job you have been doing almost all your life, persecution and afflictions, and the list goes on. How can all these things work for my good? First of all, all who are destined for greatness and who want more of God will face afflictions, but it is these afflictions God will use to mold you and bring out His perfect will in you. God did not tell Saul to persecute David, but God used it to strengthen and align significant people in David's life that helped to establish David's kingdom.

The enemy has his job, but you also have your job to do. Obviously you did not expect God to bring you into your destiny and transform you without you being an active participant in his divine will, and without a fight from the destroyer. Your job is to respond positively and play the ball that is in your court strategically and skillfully. Your job is not to panic and lose hope when your opponent is about to attack you, but to stand up and fight. If the defenders at a football or soccer game panic and lose hope, then the opponent will score an easy, uncontested goal.

Moving Forward

What obstacles are you currently facing in your life? How many times have you allowed the things you face to hold you down in depression and sadness or cause you to throw in the towel? God did not call weaklings; he called warriors. Many times we allow the obstacles to hold us down in depression and sadness; it is time you start showing the devil what you are made of and shake off the negative feelings that come to suck the very energy out of you (Hebrews 12:12-13).

Day 10
You Are Not an Accident

"Nothing in life happens by accident; that therefore means despite your present circumstances and past, you are not an accident, nor is your life meaningless."

Scriptures of the Day: Jeremiah 1: 4-10; 29: 11; Proverbs 19: 21

Discourse

Many of us live our lives with the absence of a significant person as part of our lives and growth- for example, the absence of either our father or mother. To make matters worse, there are many people who have the potential to be great men and women, but were told that their birth was by accident, that they are not important or will never accomplish anything good in life; and thus they live their lives as if their life has no meaning or purpose.

Every day a child is born and then rejected, some abandoned in bathrooms, on street corners, or at hospitals and other places. Many people faced rejection for most of their lives and feel that they do not belong anywhere, and people who they had expected to show them love only add to their rejection and low self-esteem. These rejections do not simply go away after some time, but they grow until, like an untreated sore, they began to smell and cause other problems in our lives; like a viper, they suck the very life out of us.

If you can identify with all I said before, God wants me to tell you that "YOU ARE NOT AN ACCIDENT AND YOUR LIFE HAS PURPOSE. YOU ARE SPECIAL!" I don't care what you were told and how other people made you feel at times; you are not an accident. Believe it or not, you were in the thoughts of God before he created the world, and everything you went through, and will be going through, in life, he knew and has thus given you the tools to survive, and not only survive, but to be MORE than an overcomer. You are powerful; you were wonderfully and carefully made. God took time to form you and invested gifts and abilities, wisdom, knowledge and purpose in you. Like Gideon, you are a mighty man of valor who was handpicked by God.

Everything you need is already given to you from conception. From conception he put your purpose, gifts and abilities in you so that you can be a victor and not a victim. As soon as you come to this realization, then you will realize that you are powerful. All that you have been through and all that God has invested in you has made you powerful.

Many times we spend countless hours blaming others for where our lives are now instead of looking at how we have allowed those negatives to get a hold of us, until our past and all those hurts become like parasites that suck the very life out of us until all that is left is all the hurt and pain. Well, isn't it time for a change? Our past is as big as how we made it to be. Yes, your father or mother left you at a tender age; yes, you faced rejection all your life; yes, you were sexually molested at a tender age, but that is in the past. Your future is before you; they stole your past, but are you going to let anyone steal your future? Are you going to live your life searching for pity and for handouts from others? Are you going to live your life thinking that you are weak? As a man thinketh in his heart, so is he (Proverbs 23:7). If you think you are a nobody then you will always be a nobody; if you think you have nothing positive to contribute to society, then you will forever live your life unfulfilled.

The truth is, God gave you knowledge and a brain to think for yourself. Jesus grew up in an inner city community, one of the worst anyone could grow up in, his father died at a tender age, he faced rejection all his life until the day he died, but listen to this:

JESUS DID NOT ALLOW WHERE HE CAME FROM, IIIS FAMILY BACKGROUND, WHAT OTHERS THOUGHT OR HOW THEY TREATED HIM,

OR WHAT HE HAD AND DIDN'T HAVE, TO DESTROY HIS FUTURE.

Jesus knew who he was from a tender age, and who he wasn't. He knew that he was powerful and was born for a mighty purpose. For what purpose were you born? Who are you really? Are you who people say you are? Or are you who God made you to be?

When God made man in the Garden of Eden, he made him perfect. He made man to have dominion over his territory and his future. He did not make man to walk each day like a weakling, without any purpose. When man sinned, they lost their identity. Jesus came to give back man that which they lost. Jesus died over 2000 years ago, and he restored man to their rightful position, as kings of their destiny and territory.

It's time for you to wake up in newness of life and power. It is time to change your mindset. Many people right now are living below their privilege and potential because of how they think. If you think confident, then you will walk confident. If you think you're powerful, then you will walk powerfully and command attention. If you think wealth, then you will earn wealth. But if every day you think you're a weakling, then you will live your life as a weakling. If you think you're a nobody, then you will forever be a nobody. If you think poverty, then you will forever live a life of poverty. If you think it, then you will believe it; if you believe it then you will speak it; if you speak it, then you will live it. Life and death are in the power of your tongue (Proverbs 18:21).

When God wants to bring a person to another level, the first thing He does is to change their mindset, or how they think. If He can change how they think, He will change how they operate and live their lives.

Moving Forward

As you go through this day, if your mindset is wrong, I need you to start changing how you think and view yourself and the world around you. You are not an accident; you are a miracle born to be a miracle to

someone else. God made you for a purpose, and the world is waiting on you to be who God created you to be. How you were born or how you lived your life doesn't matter; what matters is now.

Day 11
Do Not Panic; Remain Focused

"Just like the Israelites at the Red Sea and Pharaoh's army behind them, there are times the enemy will have you backed up in a death trap with nowhere to run. It is at this time you must block out all the negative words around you and listen to the voice of God. At the same time, do not panic or be afraid, but rely on God to take you through. If he brings you to your Red Sea experience, then he will open the Red Sea for you to pass through."

Scripture of the Day: Exodus 14

Discourse

The children of Israel were coming out of Egypt, where they had served as slaves for 400 years and now were set free, but not without the Lord's miraculous intervention by sending 10 plagues on Egypt. While on their way into the Promised Land, the Egyptians had a change of heart and so decided to take them back into slavery with a mighty army.

The children of Israel found themselves between a rock and a hard place with Pharaoh's vast army with chariots and weapons of war coming behind them. What were they going to do? They were defenseless and were very inexperienced in warfare, so fighting for their freedom was not an option. To add to this, they could not outrun them, as the Red Sea was before them; they were trapped- at least, in the eyes of men. Why did the Lord allow his people to be trapped when he could have stopped it from happening? As anyone of us would do, when the people saw the vast army behind them they started to panic; and of course they started to blame Moses for their situation, and murmured and complained bitterly against not only Moses, but also the Lord.

"And when Pharaoh drew nigh, the children of Israel lifted up their eyes, and, behold, the Egyptians marched after them; and they were sore afraid: and the children of Israel cried out unto the LORD. 11And they said unto Moses, Because there were no graves in Egypt, hast thou taken us away to die in the wilderness? wherefore hast thou dealt thus with us, to carry us forth out of Egypt? 12 Is not this the word that we did tell thee in Egypt, saying, Let us alone, that we may serve the Egyptians? For it had been better for us to serve the Egyptians, than that we should die in the wilderness" (Exodus 14:10-12).

The people that God miraculously delivered from of the hand of the superpower of the day, in such a manner that no other nation's god could ever have delivered its people, started to complain and wanted to go back into Egypt, which they for so long wanted to come out of. Does this sound like many of us today?

It is very important for you to understand that nothing happens by chance. God could have chosen another route for his people and could have even prevented Pharaoh from pursuing them, but he didn't, because he wanted his people to have an experience with him. I am here to tell you that, when you're in a tight situation and people want to stone or curse you, saying all manner of evil, when you are in between a rock and hard place and think you're at your lowest end, you need to block out all the negative words around you, and what people may want you to do, as your survival depends on this. Let us assume that some of children of Israel wanted to surrender to the Egyptians while some wanted to probably drown themselves in the Red Sea rather than go back into Egypt as a slave, while some where throwing hurtful words at Moses and probably the Lord; you can now imagine the position Moses was in then.

If Moses had allowed what was happening around him to throw him into a state of fright and panic, then he could not have heard the Lord saying in a state of confusion, "...lift thou up thy rod, and stretch out thine hand over the sea, and divide it: and the children of Israel shall go on dry ground through the midst of the sea" (vs 16). More important, he would not have gone to the Lord for direction in the first place; and the Lord would not have been able to destroy the enemies of Israel and bring victory in such a miraculous way to his people- an experience that stills inspires the world today and was a testament to the awesome power of God.

Moving Forward

So what am I trying to instill in you today? When you come up on your Red Sea experience and you do not know what to do or where to turn, do what Moses did:

1. Block out or ignore all the negatives around you.

2. Do not panic. If the Lord brought you to this situation, then he also has a plan to get you out.

3. Go to the Lord in prayer for direction on what you should do.

4. At all times, maintain your faith in God.

If you are at your Red Sea right now and your past seems to be catching up to you, God is able to deliver you. Perhaps your Red Sea is your finances, marital issues, problems on the job, perhaps you're facing a prison sentence; whatever may be your Red Sea, God is able to part the Red Sea from before you so that you can walk on dry land. Do not worry about your past, as the past is the past; your job is to leave the past behind you and press towards the mark of the higher calling.

Day 12
God Still Have Your Back

"Like the Israelites when they thirst for water, there will be times when we are desperate for something and are tempted to question if the Lord is with us or not; does he care and see our situation? 'Why has he led me to this area of my life?' It is at these times in our lives our relationship with him and our faith will be tested."

Scriptures of the Day: Exodus 17:1-7; Psalms 42

Discourse

Life sometimes can be so burdensome that our survival feels threatened. There will be times when our backs will be up against the wall and we can see no way out. The children of Israel were in a similar situation when they thirsted for water and all around them was deadness, no life. They were at a point in their lives where they felt helpless against the elements of their environment and had to totally rely on the grace of God.

Many of us can relate to this, as some of you reading this book right now are in a state where you feel helpless against all that is happening in your life; how many times have you been knocked down and you felt like you can't get up again? How many times have you found yourself in a situation that sometimes is not of your doing, and your back is against the wall? How many times has life thrown at you circumstances that make you feel like you want to give up on life? How many times have you found yourself in a wilderness situation?

When you find yourself in this situation, the Lord is saying to you, "Now is the time you sit down and let me handle things from here." Many times we allow life to burden us to the point where we think of committing suicide or we start questioning God, as we feel like we're not able to manage the struggles of life anymore. Guess what? God did not create us to handle life's struggles on our own. Yes, we were built to face the crises that we will face throughout our lives, but not alone; like every bridge has a support system, so is God our support system. God is never burdened by our never-ending problems, as He says that we should always cast all our cares upon Him because he cares about us (1 Peter 5:7). Your problem is never too big for God to handle.

As he did with Lazarus, sometimes the Lord wait until our situation has been giving off a bad odor for many days before he shows up. On the other hand, many times the Lord will lead us in a certain direction or place in our lives so that He may manifest his awesome power.

The children of Israel had forgotten that, even though their situation seemed impossible, they served a God that made them a promise to lead them into a prosperous land, a God who parted the Red Sea so that they could walk on dry land. When life knocks you down, get back up and fight, as God is on the job; we serve God not by sight, but by faith.

Moving Forward

As you go through this day and face your tomorrow, remember that God is always there with you. Many times we drown ourselves in afflictions, pain and all manner of life's problems because we forget who our daddy is. We trust him to handle the small issues in our lives, but when it comes to the big stuff we say to God, "God I know you are God and you helped me with my last problem, but this one is too big for you?" We think He cannot help us to pay off, or cancel that multimillion-dollar bill we have to pay, or bring back our sick family member from death. God is the God of all impossibilities. He would have not allowed certain things to happen in your life if He was not able to carry you all the way.

"Call unto me, and I will answer thee, and shew thee great and mighty things, which thou knowest not" (Jeremiah 33:3).

Day 13
Tell the Devil, No Deal

"While on our journey, sometimes the trials of life may cause us to want to give in to the demands of this world. Like Esau, we may feel tempted to sell our birthright for a promotion, sex, money, status, and other things to relieve our desires, pain and suffering or to enjoy a more fruitful life. We have to remember that what God has given us is precious because He paid for it with his own blood, not with silver or gold. He did that because we are very valuable, and He has invested greatness, strength and endurance in each one of us. Do not give in to how you feel or to the will of the world."

Scriptures of the Day: Genesis 25:29-34; Hebrews 12:1-17

Discourse

The world in which we live is filled with demanding situations such as marital and domestic issues, financial crises, job related stress, fleshly desires, health related issues, identity crises, and relationship issues, among others. Each day we are alive, we are tempted to do things that we're not supposed to, but sometimes feel helpless to stop ourselves: lie on the job, consume alcohol, follow our friends to do things we know we are not supposed to do, have sex outside of marriage, or be tempted to go after material things and pleasures of this world, among others. On top of all this, the media is not making it any easier for us, as everyday they whet our appetites with menus of how we should dress, what we should eat, or how we should live and think, and then, having done all that, garnish it with eye-catching material and sexual contents. It's no wonder that many of our youths think that if they are not driving the latest cars, going to parties, and engaging in all manner of sexual activities they have not started living as yet- after all, that's all being preached to them through the media and their friends on a daily basis.

Every day, men especially are being tempted by the physical attributes of the opposite sex, as many ladies are of the view that if they are not adorned in the shortest and tightest clothing they are not attractive enough; then they wonder why they attract guys who are only interested in having a one-night stand with them.

Every day we see people living luxurious lives while we are struggling just to get by each day, and immediately we ask, "Why am I trying to please God when that actor doesn't even pray and he is living such a blessed life? Life is ruthless." And at this point the enemy whispers in our ears, trying to deceive us and blind our eyes with things we think we need.

Esau one day came in from the field after a tired day and was very hungry. He found himself in a very tight situation where he was dying of hunger, and suddenly a birthright didn't seem so pleasing anymore, not when he was at the brink of dying, and so he sold his birthright for a morsel of meat. Many people when they are really desperate at times will even make a deal with the devil himself to get what they want- not what they really need. How many times has life backed you up in a corner, and what was wrong yesterday now seems right? How many times has the enemy thrown different things at you to knock you down? We are constantly placed in a position where we have to choose between obeying God's words or a one-night stand with that cute guy or sexy girl next door; the choice between a life of riches or staying with God.

The wrong choices always seems like a well-decorated cake, as the enemy always whets our taste buds with what our eyes can see, not the taste of the cake; he shows us the worm, but never the hook behind the worm. For many of you he may show you a life of sexual pleasure, but never how it may affect your self-image or relationship with God or the chance of pregnancy. He shows you riches and material things, but never the pain, sleepless nights and having to take sleeping pills, none of the cost of keeping your riches.

The devil is a deceiver whose only purpose is to steal what you have, kill your purpose and to destroy you (John 10:10). You may think you have nothing now, or that your life means nothing unless you have someone at your side or the latest car or gadget, or that you fly first class when you choose. Or you think that you will die in your situation unless you sell your spiritual birthright, but you are wrong. Moses decided that it was better to suffer with God than to live a life of power, fame, riches and ease. Daniel and his friends could have turned their backs on God like their fellow Jews and followed the sinful customs of Babylon, but instead they chose to stay with God. God allowed the three Hebrew boys to go into the fire because he wanted them to have an experience with God. Perhaps the temptations and trials you are presently facing are because God is about to do something in your life and if you do not go through the fire, you will not receive what God is about to give you.

But what is your birthright? In ancient times the blessings, and possessions, of the father would pass on to his children as their birthright. The first born son after the death of the father would receive a double portion of paternal inheritance, and was made the head of the family. The other children would split the rest of their father's inheritance between themselves. Esau's birthright was a blessing that would transcend all his generations to the point that they would never lack, and he gave that away for a morsel of bread when he could have easily gone into the house and ordered one of his servants to prepare something for him; Jacob was one of the richest men in the land, so how could the firstborn son die of hunger in his father's house? Our birthright may not be material blessings like what Esau had, but our birthright is our relationship with God; our birthright is our salvation. Our birthright is our purpose and gift(s). It is an inheritance that was paid for with suffering and the death of Jesus Christ. We may never live a life of abundance, but our birthright comes with the authority to command and speak things into existence. It gives us creative power; it comes with divine favor and privilege; it comes with power to change our present and future destiny.

What God has given us is more precious than what the world or anyone else can give us. Why then should any one of us settle for worldly pleasures when God is giving us the keys to the kingdom that can unlock any door, and comes with blessings (Matthew 16:19; Luke 22:29)? Why then should you settle for less than what you deserve? Everything you want is already in the kingdom and is given to you.

Moving Forward

As you go through this day, ask yourself this question: "Have I sold, or am I in the process of selling, my birthright?" If you are, then please consider, are the pleasures of this world worth you losing what God has bled and died for so that you may have an abundant life? If you are one of the few that is still holding on to God regardless of what you may face, then I encourage you to stay focused and do not sell your birthright for anything. Sex, money, and power will come at the appointed time.

"Lest there be any fornicator, or profane person, as Esau, who for one morsel of meat sold his birthright. For ye know how that afterward, when he would have inherited the blessing, he was rejected: for he found no place of repentance, though he sought it carefully with tears" (Hebrews 12:16-17).

Day 14
A Heart of Gratefulness

"Be grateful! God tested the children of Israel by giving them manna in the wilderness, but they complained and murmured against God's provision. Their murmuring and complaining led to God's anger, and his fire burnt amongst them. Forget the past and press towards the future, and whatever He lays before you, eat and be filled."

Scripture of the Day: Numbers 11

Discourse

What do you expect to find in a wilderness? A wilderness is a barren land where nothing grows and there is no water. God in His mercy and love for His people miraculously provided food and water for His people, so that they would not die of hunger on their journey.

"And the children of Israel did eat manna forty years, until they came to a land inhabited; they did eat manna until they came unto the borders of the land of Canaan" (Exodus 16: 35).

However, instead of being grateful and looking towards the future God had in store for them, they started remembering the times in Egypt when they had food to eat other than manna- a place of slavery, hardship, misery and all manner of abomination. They had the privilege of waking up each morning to find food already provided, food they did not work for, but they weren't satisfied; they wanted more and thus murmured against God's provision (Numbers 11:6, 9).

How many times has God provided for us and we, in our own way, basically pushed it back in His face, telling him like a spoiled child we do not want it? God knows that you need oxtail and shrimp dinner, but like He did with the children of Israel, God will bring us into our wilderness experience (a time of hunger, nothingness, depression, family issues, problems at work, among others) to test us to see if we will forsake Him and what was in our hearts, to show us that it is not all about the cars, house(s), the job you always wanted, family, money and material things; it is about Him, and He is our only source of survival. God does not only want us to live, but He wants us to live an abundant life (John 10:10).

God had taken his people out of bondage, but they kept looking back to Egypt instead of looking forward to what God had in store for them- the fertile land of Canaan. They were out of slavery, but their minds were still in slavery; back to a place of hardship, suffering, afflictions and abominations. It is like taking a pig out of the pig pen and putting it in a well-decorated room filled with precious things. Even though the pig is out of the pig pen, it will still behave as a pig, because mentally, it's still a pig. Their minds were not fully transformed and they could not mentally and spiritually get a hold of what God was doing, and the magnitude of what He had in store for them until their minds were fully transformed. Many of us are like that today; we were nothing, and God made us into someone that is important, but many times we act like God owes us something, or He cannot do without us. Similarly, many times He has provided for us, but instead of being grateful we speak against His provision, provisions that we did not deserve.

Before God could give them what He had in store for them, He first had to remove the mentality of Egypt out of them and renew their minds (Deuteronomy 8). The wilderness that you may be in now is not to destroy you, nor has God placed you in the wilderness because He doesn't love you; the Lord is taking you through a process. Perhaps all you can now see is a land filled with serpents and scorpions, a land of desolation and only manna to eat; however, I want you to understand that God is using your wilderness experience to mold you into the person He wants you to be so that when He is finished, you will appreciate the process and will not forsake Him. In addition, when He is finished taking you through your process, you will have the skills and wisdom you need to walk in your purpose.

God wants to bless you, but before He can bless you He must take you through your wilderness experience. Similarly, for any of us to be great, whether in the kingdom of God or in this physical world, there is a process that each one of us must go through.

We are active participants in God's divine will for us, and it is therefore up to us to decide how long it will take for us to become vessels of honor that God can be proud of. For example, if I am teaching you to ride a bicycle, I cannot determine how long it will take for you to learn to ride that bicycle. I can show you how to ride the bicycle, but at the end of the day, how quickly you master the art of riding a bicycle is totally up to you.

Moving Forward

As you go through this day and look towards the future, remember that God is always molding us so that we may be vessels of honor. He understands your situation, but He promises that He will always love you and be by your side. Furthermore, whatever provision God puts before you, be grateful. It may not be what you want, but if you remain faithful to Him and allow Him to take you through the process, then you will live an abundant life.

Day 15
Learning Trust and Obedience Through Adversities

"Striving through adversities, Jeremiah learnt to trust in the God that never fails. It was through adversities that he learnt obedience, patience, God's faithfulness, God's love, the power of God to deliver him out of situations that seems impossible, and he learnt commitment."

Scriptures of the Day: Proverbs 24: 5-12; Jeremiah 20: 7-11

Discourse

The prophet Jeremiah, in the Bible, was called to proclaim God's words to a rebellious and wicked generation, a generation that had the form of God but was far away from him- Judah (the southern kingdom). At the time Jeremiah was called to be a prophet from a very tender age, society was at a stage similar to ours today: society was deteriorating economically, politically, and spiritually. It was a time when wars and captivity were the order of the world scene, and God's words were deemed offensive to His people. Despite the condition of God's people, and the knowledge that speaking in God's name could make him one of the most hated men and treated as a traitor to his people, Jeremiah faithfully confronted the leaders and people about their sins. Even after Jerusalem fell and he was forcefully taken to Egypt, Jeremiah remained faithful to God in a land of adultery, idol worshipping and wickedness.

The will and calling of God upon our lives will not always be easy. Your trust in God will be tested very often, and it is at these times you will be forced to remember and rely on the promises of God in your life. Many times, like the prophet Jeremiah, we may cry unto God, saying, 'Lord, you have deceived me, because I thought by doing your will people would accept me, but instead I've become a laughing stock; even my own friends have forsaken me.' It will not always be easy to serve God, but if we stay strong, keep our focus, walk in the STRENGTH OF THE LORD, then in the end all things will work out for our good. Jeremiah was vindicated in the end and all his enemies were ashamed (after over 15 years).

All of us can relate to Jeremiah- living in a world that desperately seeks material things, a world where morality has broken down and what was once wrong is now made to be right, what was once shunned is now looked upon as ideal; a world where people have forsaken the true and living God to go after the god of money, sex, material things, education and other worldly pursuits; where they have a form of Godliness but are not allowing God to direct their steps. Many people want the blessings and everything God can give them, but not God. They will say they want and worship God, but what they actually mean is that they occasionally attend church, pray sometimes and praise God when things are going well in their lives. They say they are serving God faithfully, but their lives are saying they have someone else other than the creator as their God.

We can all learn something from Jeremiah's life. Despite the unfaithfulness of God's people, he remained faithful and obedient to every command of God- even the ones that could have caused him to lose his life, those that would arouse the laughter and ridicule of even his closest friends and family members (e.g. Jeremiah 27:2). Jeremiah learnt that God will always keep His promises, but He never said how He will keep them. God's calling on his life had seem very enticing at the beginning, but God never told Jeremiah that to do his work, he would in the middle of his ministry cry out unto God, saying:

"O LORD, you have deceived me, and I was deceived. You overpowered me and won. I've been made fun of all day long. Everyone mocks me. Each time I speak, I have to cry out and shout, "Violence and destruction!" The word of the LORD has made me the object of insults and contempt all day long. I think to myself, "I can forget the LORD and no longer speak his name." But his word is inside me like a burning fire shut up in my bones. I wear myself out holding it in, but I can't do it any longer. I have heard many people whispering, "Terror is everywhere! Report him! Let's report him!" All my closest friends are waiting to see me stumble. They say, "Maybe he will be tricked. Then we can overpower him and take revenge on him" (Jeremiah 20:7-10) (Gods Words translation).

Jeremiah could say with great certainty, "The LORD is on my side like a terrifying warrior. That is why those who persecute me will stumble. They can't win. They will be very ashamed that they can't succeed. Their eternal shame will not be forgotten" (vs 11).

Do not allow the negatives, persecution and trials you face to deter you from moving forward in your career, family life, ministry, Christian pathway, and life in general; the things that face you are there to strengthen you. When the people were taken captive and naked to Babylon, Jeremiah was spared. When many people were dying of hunger, Jeremiah was fed. When the people were in a state of fear and hopelessness, Jeremiah was comforted and filled with hope in God's provision and promises.

Moving Forward

As you go through this day and face the rest of your life, please remember that at times we may think of giving up because of disappointments, rejections, and persecutions which may bring us to a point of despondency, but this is not the time to throw in the towel as God still have work for you to do; someone is in need of your gift.

Day 16
You Are a Mustard Seed

"Except a corn of wheat fall into the ground and die, it abideth alone; but if it die, it bringeth forth much fruit. In order for God to get the glory out of you and in order for you to do mighty things for God, you must go through the process, your flesh must die"-John 12:24

Scripture of the Day: Matthew 13:31-32

Discourse

Have you ever read or heard about the parable of the mustard seed? Jesus said unto his followers:

"The kingdom of heaven is like a mustard seed, which a man took and planted in his field. Though it is the smallest of all seeds, yet when it grows, it is the largest of garden plants and becomes a tree, so that the birds come and perch in its branches" (Matthew 13:31-32).

Notice, the seed is the smallest seed in the world, but this same seed grew to be a very mighty tree so that birds of the air could be sheltered by it. Some of you are seen by others as insignificant, a nobody, while some of you have been thrown down to the ground and stepped on as someone steps on a piece of trash, and some of you people have been thrown into emotional garbage bins and forgotten about. But the thing I love about the parable of the mustard seed is the end. Before the mustard tree could become one of the most important trees in the forest, it first had to be buried in the ground; it then goes through a process where it is watered by the rain and the sun shines upon it, giving it the energy to grow. In a similar manner, God has allowed the enemy (using people around us) to bury some of you in despair, low self-esteem, emotional and psychological turmoil, and then as if all of those weren't enough, to be trampled upon and then discarded like a piece of trash.

But did you know that all you have been through and are currently going through is to qualify you for your purpose?

All you have been through is to make you an instrument of deliverance and to make you great- this is supposed to make you start jumping up right now with unspeakable joy. God has used all those things you have been through to form a key of deliverance and healing, and a key of power in your hand to destroy everything the enemy has set up in the lives of people around the world; yes, your trials qualify you for an international ministry.

I want to tell you right now that you are that mustard seed that God is preparing to bloom, and when he is ready to exalt you, the same people that spit upon you and treat you as a nobody, the same people that trample you will be running to you for advice, prayer, for a job, a recommendation, and to ask for help. God will make them your footstool and prepare a table before your enemies. Not only that, but He will use you to deliver people who are deep in self-pity, people who are dying inside and are ready to throw in the towel. You are that mustard seed that will shelter and feed the depressed, persecuted, and all those in need of a word that will take them to the next level in ministry and or life.

Samson killed more in his death than when he was alive; his true strength was manifested when they thought he was no more of a threat to them. For God to flex His muscles in us and for our true potential to manifest, we first have to die to the things of this world; our flesh must die so that our spirit may live.

Moving Forward

As you go through this day and face all those things that are thrown at you, please consider that everyone who has belittled and trampled you under their feet, and all you have been through because of people, they have given you a gold spoon without them knowing. They thought you would not have made it and would never come to anything good, but what they were not counting on is the God behind your struggles; they did not know that God was preparing you so that He may exalt you. You are a miracle sent by God to be a miracle to someone else.

Day 17
What is your Response?

"Your reaction to your circumstances proves to the enemy who you put your trust in and who your God is. Paul and Silas were thrown in prison, and not only that, but they were locked in a dungeon, but they did not allow their present situation to dictate how they felt spiritually and otherwise. Instead of burying themselves in depression, at midnight they started praising God and God showed up mightily in their situation."

Scripture of the Day: Acts 16: 16-40

Discourse

Some of you, the enemy has thrown you in a prison, not only in the prison of despair, hopelessness, abuse, rejection, heartaches, financial depression, marital and other family issues, children giving you problems, drug and alcohol abuse, sexual promiscuity amongst others, but he went two steps further and has put you in the inner prison and then chained your feet so that it is impossible for you to escape. He thought this would be the end of you; but he was wrong.

Did you know that some of the most dangerous people on earth are the ones that feel like they have lost everything and are down in the pit with no way out? Let's look at it another way: the most dangerous boxer in a ring is not the one that is winning, but it is the one that is knocked down and feels as if this is it for him now, he is dead, he cannot sink any further or be in a worse condition than he is now in. When the enemy has you knocked down on the ground and it seems like there is no way out of your situation- you have sunk so far in depression, drugs and all different kinds of abuse, neglect, low self-esteem, depression etc., the only thing left for you to do is to make one last attempt at survival. The boxer who is knocked down and believes he is already dead has only one option before he loses everything- with all strength he has, he can get up and take one last swing at his opponent with everything he has. If you can relate to this, you need to look the enemy in his face and say, "Devil, I am down right now, but I am not going down by myself, I am taking you with me. There is no way I am dying today and you don't have any injury on your body. I am going to die, but I am taking you with me." That is the deadliest blow.

Some of you, the enemy thinks he has you, it's the end of your ministry, your marriage, you will never go back to school or get out of poverty, your children will all die by the gun, you will never rise again, your family is over, you will never become anything good in life, your vision will never come to pass. The enemy thought he killed Joseph's dream when he had him sold as slave in Egypt, but what he did not know is that by sending Joseph as slave in Egypt, then throwing him in prison, he was actually positioning him with the right people and setting him up for greatness, for the pit was just a foundation for his elevation. Look at your situation and start giving God some crazy praise like you have never praised him before, because you are not coming out empty handed- you are coming out with great treasures.

The praise that Paul and Silas gave God at midnight- your midnight represents whatever heartaches or trouble that have you locked up in despair and threaten to destroy you, or someone you care about- it's your pit- was the greatest praise they ever gave to God throughout their entire ministry; they had never praised God like that before. They should have been depressed and wondering why God suffered them to be put in prison; they were probably expecting death, as that was the penalty for introducing another religion that was not sanctioned by the Roman government. Instead of saying their last prayers and throwing in the towel, they gave God the greatest praise they had ever given him to the point that God was moved by their praise and did something extraordinary. Their praise shook the foundation of the prison; not only that, but all those who were held captive were set free. I want to tell you right now that the enemy has positioned you to lose some people that the enemy has held captive for years, and all you have to do is just praise God. Praise him with everything that is in you.

Moving Forward

As you go through this day, consider the situation Paul and Silas were in- a situation that should have had them killed. What the enemy meant for your destruction, God will turn it around for your good and give you a testimony. Your testimony and praise will give someone life and take many out of bondage. Do not despair because of your current situation, as it's not an indication of your future, but just start giving God some praise and worship and see the Lord work in your situation.

Part 2

Dealing With Self and Others

Day 18
Following God Even When it Hurts

"The Lord our God is the Lord of host; he is our shepherd (guide, provider and protector). The Lord never promises us that what he ask us to do sometimes will not sound and look foolish; for example, it looked and probably sounded foolish for Joshua to march around Jericho's wall for 6 days saying and doing nothing. At times we will be laughed at, called a fool, misunderstood, etc. for God, but there is a reward in obeying the commands of the Lord."

Scriptures of the Day: Mark 9: 1-7; Joshua 7: 12-21

Discourse

At times the Lord will ask us to do things that will seem foolish to the human eye. Too many times, we tend to put God in a box and say God must operate in a certain manner, but I want you to understand that God is not confined to your human thinking, your program, or by how He did things in the days of the prophets or apostles. When Jesus told the mourners that were mourning over Jairus' dead daughter that she was not dead, but asleep, he sounded and looked foolish (Mark 5:21-43), and was probably called a madman when "he spat on the ground, and made clay of the spittle, and he anointed the eyes of the blind man with the clay" (John 9:6). When Jesus was upon earth, oftentimes when he said and did things he was ridiculed, but in the end they started glorifying God for the 'foolish' things he did.

Jesus and the apostles proved over and over that you cannot simply 'lock God in a box' and say this is how he will work, and what he will do and not do; but at the same time you must ensure that what is being done and said does not contradict the Bible.

There will be times when the Lord will ask you to do something that will put you in harm's way or to do something that will cause you to be ridiculed by those around you. However, if you want to be in ministry and work for God, you must be prepared to be ridiculed and persecuted for the Word of the Lord. You will feel fearful at times, but if God gives you a task to perform, then He will give you the strength to perform His command, and He will be with you.

Moving Forward

As you go through this day, let each one of us be fully persuaded in our minds that we will follow God no matter what may come- even when we are laughed at, talked about, afflicted by others, forsaken, belittled, and mistreated amongst others. The apostles went through much persecution, and now they are awaiting their heavenly reward. You too will be heavily rewarded if you faint not.

Day 19
Forsaken by People, Accepted by God

"There are times in your life when people will turn their backs on you as if you are not important and don't mean anything to them. When this happens, though it may be hard, do not become distressed or become hateful, as sometimes God is just processing you and making you stronger."

Scriptures of the Day: Mark 14: 29-50; Isaiah 53:3

Discourse

We are all social beings created to be in the company of those whom we love; therefore, all of us like to believe that we can always count on friends and or family. We all want to have the confidence that the person(s) we care about and or see as important also see us as significant and care about us. The truth is, life doesn't always work as we like it to. There will be times in our lives when people we care about, when we've always been there for them, always attended to their every need, when we need them the most, they are not there for us. There will be times when we feel forsaken, cast down and insignificant in the eyes of those around us, even by people who were always there for us. What do you do when this happens? Do you start crying, or do you pick yourself up and move on? Do you hate the other person(s) and stop caring about him/her/them?

When Jesus was upon the earth he was rejected, persecuted and often felt alone. Some of the same people whom he delivered from sickness and demonic oppression turned their backs on him; even his own disciples, when he was held for treason, deserted him.

What do you do then when all hell breaks loose and there is no one to call upon? When the people who matter to you most are not available over the phone or in person to even ask if you are okay?

The true test of a man's character is not when everything is going well in his life and people are showering him with affection, but it is when he feels rejected and forsaken by those he cares most about and can still love them. His true character will show when they treat him as if he is not important and he can still shower them with affection and love.

God will sometimes take you out of your comfort zone so that He may groom you for your purpose. To do this, sometimes the Lord will allow rejection, persecution, and loneliness so that He may build and test you to see how you will react when different situations arise.

David, before he could sit upon the throne of Israel, was rejected and treated as a criminal running for his life by the king whom he held in high regard. Every great man before God exalted them went through a period of rejection and loneliness. How will you handle power if there is any root of bitterness in your heart? God therefore put you through a process so that He may test and build you.

Additionally, He will put you through a time when people belittle and speak hurtful words against you, so that He may build your character for when the true test of persecutions come.

Will you run from the process, or will you embrace it? Will you allow how people treat and speak to you to cause you to lose focus of where God is taking you and who you are? Remember, you cannot render evil for evil done to you, because you are not like everyone else. God is building you for greatness, and sometimes where God is taking you, some people cannot come. Some people only come into your life for a short period of time to teach you something, so don't try to hold unto them when their purpose has been accomplished.

Moving Forward

As you go through this day and move forward in life, always try to remember that rejection and loneliness is a part of the process each one of us must go through. It will be rough, but you must endure it and come out as pure gold. At times, the Lord will take some people out of your life so that you may focus on Him and be the person He wants you to be.

Day 20
Be Careful of Who You Associate Yourself With

"If you continue to surround yourself with negative people and influences, then you will never rise to your full potential or become who God calls you to be."

Scriptures of the Day: 1 Corinthians 5; Proverbs 16: 29

Discourse

Jesus saw a man at the pool of Bethesda one day sitting with the lame, the crippled, and the blind; he was there for 38 years in the same position, doing the same thing repeatedly and still in the same depressive, paralyzing state, getting the same results and hanging out with the same people waiting for the moving of the water, waiting day after day, year after year for his breakthrough. Jesus asked the man, 'Will thou be made whole? I notice you have been in this same situation for 38 years, but do you want to be healed, do you want to have a new life, do you want your life to be whole? I want to deliver you from the life you have been living, but I am not going to give you what I have for you unless you want it. I am not going to touch you, but if you want it, then you can have it.' The man in response to Jesus' question replied, "Sir, I have no man, when the water is troubled, to put me into the pool: but while I am coming, another steppeth down before me" (John 5:7).

Jesus did not ask him the reason he was not healed, but if he wanted to be made whole. Isn't it interesting that when you have been in the same situation for many years and hanging out with certain people, after a while you start thinking and acting like them?

The crippled man at the pool had lost hope. Thirty eight years of doing the same thing and getting the same results. Thirty eight years of hanging around the same people, people that could not help him, folks that were sick and in need of help. He was in one stage of his life for thirty eight years; never moving to the next level of his life and not realizing when his breakthrough was right before him, because he allowed his thinking to be corrupted by his situation and the people he hung around. He got frustrated and lost hope of ever getting well because of his thinking. His thinking controlled his behavior. He was in a place of deliverance and healing, but his atmosphere was of emotional death.

That is what will happen when you hang around negative people and allow negative thoughts to shape your perspective and influence your decisions. Many people are in church, or in the same job doing the same thing for years and fail to move to the next level of ministry and life because of who they allowed to control their space- our space means our mind and our environment. Similarly, many marriages and families are broken because of outside influences. Who is it you are allowing to control your mind? Who are you listening to and hanging out with? Spirits are transferable. What that means is if you hang around folks that are not seeking after God, folks that are backstabbers and gossipers, folks that go to church for the sole purpose of hooking up with guys or girls, folks that skip classes, and the list goes on, then the same attitude they have is the same attitude you will manifest.

Have you ever wondered why, when you hang around some people that gossip, after a while you start to gossip and enjoy doing it? Spirits are transferable. If you continue to hang around and listen to negative people, people whose lives are stagnant, then you will never grow to your full potential in God, and in life as a whole. God cannot take you to another level in ministry, or cause you to excel at school or in your job unless you change how you think and how you think control your life. One of the greatest hindrances to many people not moving to another level in their career, ministry, education, or life is not because they do not have what it takes to move to another level, but it's because of those who they associate themselves with. Spirits are transferable.

God told the children of Israel that when they enter Canaan they should utterly destroy everyone they see in the land. Why? Israel will follow their customs and practices and thus pollute their minds with their way of thinking and lifestyle.

Moving Forward

It is impossible to live a life that is unaffected by other people. Many times we allow their attitudes and opinions, like pollen, to blow into our lives, shaping our perspective and influencing our decisions. However, it is our responsibility to be careful of the people we associate ourselves with and allow to get in our space- our mind. For you to grow, you will have to leave certain company and seek after God. I am in no way saying you should stop talking to them altogether; what I am saying is be careful of who you allow to get in your territory, who you listen to and hang out with.

Have a blessed day.

Day 21
Do Not be Afraid of Their Faces

"The apostles knew that if they should preach anything about Jesus, their lives would be endangered by the religious leaders of their day; yet they never refrained from obeying God. Do not be afraid of their faces, nor should you let the words of others hinder you from doing the will of God. If you stand and do his will, God will always deliver you. Nothing can happen to you unless God says so. Who is man that you should be mindful of him? Let not fear cripple your purpose."

Scriptures of the day: St. John 15:20; Acts 4:1-3, 13-22

Discourse

Many times, we allow the perception, attitude, words and or behavior of those around us to hinder us from doing what God commanded us to do. Many gifts, ministries, dreams and visions are aborted because of the words and attitudes of others. If Jesus or the apostles had allowed the religious and secular people of their day to hinder or stop them from completing their task, then none of us would be here right now. You and I are here because few men decided to take a stand and do their job.

What task has the Lord handed to you, at work or at church, that you are afraid of doing because of what others may say or do? Fear is not of God for he has not given us the spirit of fear but of power to do what he commanded us to do (2 Timothy 1:7). Perhaps you have to talk to someone and you are afraid of doing so, or perhaps you have a talent you are afraid of showing as you think people may laugh at you. Perhaps it is fear of sharing your thoughts at the workplace, school or church. Whatever it may be, remember this: someone right now is depending on what you have to say or do. Some may not appreciate you, but that is because what you have to say or do will not benefit them. Sometimes

God will send you to speak to a crowd just to meet one person. Not everyone in your job, ministry or church will like you or stand with you, but do not lose any sleep over them; many people will fight against you because they are jealous or afraid of the anointing that is upon your life. Those who are busy moving up in ministry and otherwise do not have time to criticize or belittle others; instead, they try to bring others up with them.

While others were too busy seeking ways to destroy Jesus and the apostles, they were too busy occupying themselves with the things of God and living their life to the plan and will of God. They delivered the messages God gave them and moved on. Whoever wanted to love and accept them, they gave God thanks; whoever rejected the Word of God and them, they moved on without holding any grudge or hating those who opposed them.

Moving Forward

As you go through this day, resolve in your mind that you will not allow the faces and words of others to stop you from living your life to the will of God; nor will you be afraid to carry out the command of God. The prophets and apostles of old were mistreated, humiliated, called awful names, and beaten, among other things, but they endured all things, and we count them happy who had endured.

Day 22
The Most Powerful Weapon You Have

"When the enemies of King Jehoshaphat came upon him with a vast army, the first thing he did was not to assemble his army, but he gathered the people together and they went before the Lord in prayer. Because he did not rely on men, but on God, he did not even have to lift one sword against his enemies; instead, he worshipped, and his enemies were confounded and turned against each other. Worship is one of the most powerful weapons we have at our disposal. When the enemy and our problems come upon us, let us first go to the Lord in prayer, in faith and worship."

Scripture of the day: 2 Chronicles 20:1-13, 22-25

Discourse

Many times when we are confronted with situations and circumstances, the first thing we do is not to take the matter to the Lord in prayer, but we start to worry and or complain, then we try to deal with the matter on our own. If all our efforts fail, we try to invite God into a situation that has gotten out of control or become unmanageable. We forget that the Bible says in Matthew 11:28, "Come unto me, all ye that labour and are heavy laden, and I will give you rest." And, in 1 Peter 5:7, "Casting all your care upon him; for he careth for you."

God does not want us to take care of our problems outside of him; nor does He want us to call upon Him for help when the situation has gotten out of control. Instead, He wants us to do like Jehoshaphat and consult Him about everything first; in everything we do, we are to consult Him before we attempt to do anything.

I remember I went to the Lord about going back to University to complete my studies and He said yes, He would help me. Armed with a direct word of assurance from the Lord, and trying to prove my faith in God and His promise, I went ahead and applied for my master's degree without knowing how I was going to fund my first tuition payment. I thought I could go ahead and apply because He promised He would help me. The problem was, I did not ask Him when I should apply or how I should go about making my next move; nor did I have His assurance that if I should apply at that particular time, He'd help with the financial aspect of my studies. I was of the impression that if I went ahead and applied I was expressing my faith in God (at that time I was trying to understand what it meant to have faith in God). I ended up in financial troubles because of my action.

Not every time the Lord gives us a promise should we run ahead of His appointed time, as there is an appointed for everything. I have learnt that oftentimes, He will give you a promise without telling you when the promise will come to pass, just as He did with Abraham. God made Abraham a promise that his wife Sarah shall bear a child, but God did not tell him that he would have to wait over 20 years for the promise to be fulfilled; and like Abraham, I tried to help God. God does not need our help to accomplish His work; all he needs is our faith in His spoken or written words and for us to do our part.

Moreover, there will be times in our lives when we face tough situations that seek to destroy our very existence; or we may face circumstances that will cause us to question who we are, why we are here, our purpose, and if God is really there with us. It is in these times our faith will be tested, but we must do as Jehoshaphat did, when he maintained his trust in God even when he was facing an army that could wipe out his kingdom in few hours (2 Chronicles 20:1-2). Oftentimes we allow the situations we face to burden us to the point where we simply cannot function in our daily life- family life suffers, our ministry suffers, our education suffers, our job suffers, and even our worship suffers as we allow circumstances to burden our mind. Consequently, many of us become physically sick, not because of any physical ailment, but because of stress. Worrying about the different problems we face can be compared to us telling God, 'I know you came through for me last time, but Lord, I am now in a situation that is too big for you.' Worry is therefore the opposite of faith. If I trust you to carry my bag across the road, then I will go about my business knowing you have everything under control. I therefore have faith in your capabilities to do the task I asked you to do.

When situations come upon us, God wants us to do the opposite of worrying. He wants us to leave everything to Him and worship Him for what He is about to do. Worship is telling God that despite what I am going through or what is happening, you deserve to be worshipped. 'Lord, I know the facts says I will never get well, my kids will never attend university, I will never be free from drug addiction, but Lord, your Word says healing is the children's bread; your Word says you will provide all my needs; your Words says blessings shall overtake me, so Lord, I am leaving everything in your hand.' I don't care what the facts are, God is able to deliver you, and if He can't, then He is not God. When creation worships the creator, God will always show up, as God inhabits the worship and praise of His people; when God sees your faith, He will magnify Himself in your life.

If Jehoshaphat and the people of Judah did not worship, God would not have destroyed their enemies without them lifting one sword. God is therefore saying to us that all He wants us to do is to worship Him out of our situation. When we worship and praise God, angels literally go to battle fighting on our behalf. Everything that happens on earth must first happen in the spiritual realm; it is a battle that we are not able to see with our natural eyes. We only see the result of the unseen battle being manifested in our lives. Judah did not see the battle being fought in the spirit; they only came to take away the spoil in abundance that took them three days to carry (2 Corinthians 20: 22-25). God is about to give some to you at the end of the crisis you are facing in your life; an increase in blessing that you will not have room to contain.

Moving Forward

As you go through this day and face life's burdens, remember that God is with you. The Lord does not need much to fight your battles or to lift your burdens; all He needs at times is your faith and for you to worship with all your heart, despite what you may be going through. As smoke is driven by the wind, so God shall drive away your problems.

Day 23
Press Through the Obstacles Standing Before You

"Sometimes to reach God or receive what God has for you, you must go through a wall of flesh, including your own. Despite the disapproval and murmurings of Jesus' disciples, Mary pressed her way through a wall of flesh to worship at Jesus' feet. Whenever you are in a hostile, depressive, and contrary environment, and whenever you want something from God, do not murmur, fight or complain; just worship God and see what God will do."

Scriptures of the day: Mark 14:1-9; John 12: 3

Discourse

The Bible shows us a rare occasion of what it means to overcome obstacles put in our way by people that are in position when it talks about Mary, who washed Jesus' feet with her tears and wiped his feet with her hair. It shows us that there will be times when our hearts are bursting with sorrows and we need to pour it out at the feet of Jesus; but there will be roadblocks, walls of flesh that we will need to destroy. The wall of flesh, or obstacle in Mary's path, was Jesus' disciples.

The Bible says that while Jesus was in Bethany in the house of Simon the leper, as he was reclining at a table, a woman came with an alabaster box of ointment of spikenard, very costly, and she broke the box and poured it on his head. There were some who said indignantly, "'Why was the ointment wasted like that? For this ointment could have been sold for more than three hundred denarii and given to the poor.' And they scolded her" (Mark 14:3-5).

Mary's determination to anoint the head and wipe his feet with her hair should be a sign and example to all of us that, whenever we are trying to worship God for our breakthrough, at times there will be murmuring from people around us who will want to stop us either physically, or with their mouths from receiving our breakthrough or a Word from the

Lord- even from people in the clergy (pastors and other ministers of the gospel).

Additionally, the story of Mary shows us that we will not always have it easy when we are trying to accomplish a given goal, as there will be oppositions. Perhaps your goal may be to get a doctoral degree, plan an event at your workplace, to get married, or even to obey a command from the Lord- there will be people who will talk. Mary realized this, but she knew what she was about and that at the end of the day she was the one who needed her breakthrough, not Jesus' disciples; therefore, she pushed her way through a thick wall of flesh and washed the feet of Jesus. As she stepped through the door she could feel that she was not welcome, as she was seen as an outcast, being a prostitute, a sinner woman who had no right to go before the master. Yes, she was scared, but she mustered enough courage and did what she had to do.

What obstacles stand in your way of you accomplishing your dream(s), becoming who God says you are, or walking in your purpose? You may see a thick wall before you and your dream/purpose is on the other side, and you may say to yourself, 'This wall standing before me is too thick for me to go through or break down,' or 'This, what I am facing, is too much for me to handle, I might as well throw in the towel.' But aren't you tired of throwing in the towel? Haven't you had enough of seeing other people walking in their purpose, some of the same people standing in your way, and you are not? Well if you are, then it's time you muster enough strength and break down the wall standing before you. God knows you cannot do this on your own, so that is why He says, "My grace is sufficient for thee: for my strength is made perfect in (your) weakness" (2 Corinthians 12:9).

When the Israelites came out of the wilderness and went into the Promise Land, they could not just go up and possess the land God had given them; they had to totally destroy all the inhabitants that were occupying the land. The first enemy they faced was the people of Jericho. This was an easy task for the Israelites, as God was fighting their battles. However, there was an obstacle before them; the city of Jericho was surrounded by a thick wall they did not have the tools to breakdown. They didn't have bulldozers like we do today that could break down walls. They could have lost all hope of ever occupying the land God gave them, but they did not. Instead of losing all hope, their leader Joshua went to the Lord for direction and He told Joshua to let the people march around the wall of Jericho once (1) for six (6) days, and on the seventh (7) day they were to march around the wall seven (7) times and then the people were to shout when they heard the blowing of the trumpet. The Israelites must have been mocked and ridiculed by the inhabitants of Jericho, and perhaps some of the Israelites must have thought that the command of Joshua was very foolish. Walking around a city once per day without making a single sound must have looked, and felt, very foolish, but they obeyed. When the Israelites marched around the city seven times on the last day and shouted, God did something that he never did before: the walls of Jericho fell down flat and the children of Israel were able to enter the city and destroy all the inhabitants of the land.

What am I trying to say to you? I am saying if you are bold enough to do the unexpected, then you shall have your shout in the end, and the thick wall that stands before you shall fall down flat. You shall have your victory; you shall overcome.

Sometimes you will even have to go against the order of the day or disrupt the status quo. The disciples had gotten comfortable with Jesus and how things were going. They had always had Jesus around them, so to make an effort to impress him was not on their agenda. They, like many people in the church today, are comfortable in having church as usual...until...a woman that was seen as a nobody and should not be in 'church', much less to touch Jesus, decided that she was not going to leave until she got Jesus' attention and received her deliverance. What she did changed the atmosphere.

I will not say it will be easy, as sometimes the enemy will stand up as a tall wall before you, trying to stop you from reaching God, but you have to look at the wall before you and say, 'What is this Great Wall that stands before me? You shall fall flat like the wall of Jericho.'

Perhaps your wall is how you are perceived and treated by those around you, or perhaps your wall is your family, your community, your social status, your level of education, or how you perceived yourself, your abilities and self-worth; whatever your wall is, God is calling you to another level. God is asking you to break down the wall standing in your way from seeing Him clearly, and being whom He created you to be. Perhaps the wall standing before you is the atmosphere of the church which you attend. Each of us is anointed to change our situation and the atmosphere around us.

God wants me to write this book to tell you that if you are willing enough to challenge the wall that is before you, then He will fight your battles. If you are willing enough, He will do what you thought was impossible and not only break down your Jericho wall, but He will consume it with fire.

Moving Forward

As you go through this day, what wall stands before you right now? Is it your own flesh and how you perceive your own self-worth? Is it the people around you? Perhaps it's your past. Whatever it may be, ask yourself this question: 'Am I willing to go through the 'roof' or press through a crowd to see a move of God? Am I willing to push through the negatives I have been hearing all my life? Am I willing enough to break the wall down by whatever means necessary so I can become that doctor, minister of the gospel, pilot, educator, business owner, CEO of a Fortune 500 company, or that lawyer I always wanted to be?'

You are anointed to be whatever God calls you to be. You are anointed to change your present situation. You are anointed to change the atmosphere of your church, family, community and country. Challenge your wall!! If you can challenge it, then you can break it down

Day 24
Treat Others with Respect

"Do not spend your life looking down on or belittling others, mistreating or speaking evil of others because the tables can easily be turn. Moreover, the one you mistreated or looked down at today, may be the one you cry to for help tomorrow."

Scriptures of the Day: Galatians 6: 7-10; Matthew 9: 9-13

Discourse

Many times we mistreat, belittle, talk down at, or don't pay someone much attention, probably because they didn't have much to offer us, or we thought they weren't important, or for any other selfish reason, not realizing that the table may easily be turned tomorrow in their favor.

Let's   illustrate:
A teacher may have a boy in his or her class that is not performing very well, misbehaves at times, and doesn't pay much attention in class; on top of all that, he is seen as the 'worst' student in the class, probably in the whole school. Everyone thinks he will not come to anything good in the future, but will live the rest of his life as a worthless child, maybe a criminal. The teacher may speak hurtful words to that child: 'You will never come to anything good in life,' 'You're worthless and I won't waste my time on teaching you.' The child wants to learn and to do better, but the child doesn't know how, but all the teacher does instead of helping that child is to belittle and ignore that child.

When he was 17 years old he met a teacher who gave him the opportunity to turn his life around. As life would have it, that child who no one paid any attention to and thought he would not come to anything good in life ultimately became a well-respected doctor, the author of many books and operated his own hospital. The same person no one thought would amount to anything in life, was mistreated and looked down on, became one of the most sought after doctors in his field.

What is the point I am trying to make? Treat everyone you come in contact with respect. Never look down at or belittle, speak negative words against, or mistreat anyone. Instead, treat everyone in a respectable manner and in the way you would like them to treat you. As much as it lies in you, give equal opportunity to everyone. That person you spoke evil against or looked down on may be the very one who holds your life in his or her hand when you are battling for life in the hospital.

If you are someone who is being mistreated, belittled, or spoken to in a disrespectful and or hurtful manner, I encourage you not to be discouraged, but hold your head high; know who you are and never let anyone, regardless of their position, make you think or feel that you are not important or powerful, and that you will never be great. Remember, God died so that you may have life and live your life to the fullest.

You are worth much more than what people may think, or even you may think. You may think that you're no one of importance, but I am here to tell you that greatness lies within you. Jesus suffered much hunger, humiliation and sorrow so that you may walk this world with power and the knowledge that your life means something. You are not who your friends, family, and those you come in contact with think or say you are; but you are who God says you are.

So   what   should   you   do?

1. Stop entertaining the thoughts that you are not important and you are not powerful. As a man thinks, so is he (Proverbs 27:3). God made you to be the head and not the tail; above and not beneath; a conqueror and not live a defeated and miserable life; nor did He create you to be a slave to the elements or things of this world.

2. Think of yourself as royalty, because you are a child of the King of all

Kings and walk as such. As a king, God made you to rule your domain [your thoughts & your environment], the physical realm, and the spiritual realm. The bible says:

The heaven, even the heavens, are the LORD'S: but the earth hath he given to the children of men" (Psalms 115: 16).

"What is man, that thou art mindful of him? and the son of man, that thou visitest him?

For thou hast made him a little lower than the angels, and hast crowned him with glory

and honour. Thou madest him to have dominion over the works of thy hands; thou hast

put all things under his feet: All sheep and oxen, yea, and the beasts of the field;

The fowl of the air, and the fish of the sea, and whatsoever passeth through the paths of the seas" (Psalms 8:4-8:7).

When God created man he created them to "replenish the earth, and subdue it: and have dominion over the fish of the sea, and over the fowl of the air, and over every living thing that moveth upon the earth" (Genesis 1:28).

Take back your position and let no one move you.

3. Do not hate or hold any grudge against anyone. Let no ill feeling creep up or linger in your heart against anyone. Let love, peace and joy fill your heart.

4. If you belittle or oftentimes speak evil words against or to anyone, stop immediately. Treat and speak to others as you would want to be treated or spoken to.

Moving Forward

As you go through this day and face the rest of your life, remember that no one is created more important than anyone else; all of us are created equal, with different roles to play. No one else can play your part or be you; you are special. Each one of us was created for a very important purpose. The person you meet today may be the person God sends to bless you or bring you further in your life or ministry regardless of how that person may look, smell or that person's educational or social background. Have a blessed day!

Part 3

Facing Oppositions

Day 25

Face and Overcome Your Own Flesh

"Sometimes in order to become who God says you are, to have victory in the midst of your situation, hope in the midst of hopelessness, and deliverance in a contrary environment, you must be willing to go through a wall of flesh, including yours."

Scriptures of the Day: Luke 8: 43-48; Mark 2: 1-12; 14: 1-9

Discourse

The biggest and hardest enemy to identify, fight and destroy is our own flesh. We are our own destroyer and hindrance to our growth and deliverance at times.

The woman with the issue of blood was caught between a rock and a hard place. On one hand, she was faced with a very expensive and embarrassing issue for twelve years and had lost all hope of being healed when she met Jesus by 'accident'. The normal period for women to have their monthly menstrual period is 3 to 5 days; this woman had hers for 12 years. In ancient Israel when a woman starts having her monthly menstrual period she had to be separated from her children, husband, family and the entire community, as she was seen as unclean. Everything she touched and everyone who touched her became unclean. It is a situation that prevented her from enjoying the pleasures of life that we take for granted, like simply touching someone, walking in the market, laying on the bed with someone and so on. For 12 years she could not hold or touch her child; her husband could not cuddle her and show her any affection. For 12 years she lived a life of separation filled with depression, and with very little hope. Perhaps her condition left her without any money, as the Bible says she spent all she had on medical bills without any positive change in her condition. When she met Jesus she was at the 'end of the rope', perhaps she felt like this was it now- I am going to kill myself. Can you imagine having an issue for 12 years that prevents you from enjoying the simple things of life, like touching? Yes, I know women having their menstrual cycle in today's society can touch their loved ones and are not seen as unclean; but this was not the case with women living in Israel at the time, as according to their religious law, she was unclean. A normal part of being a woman that should have lasted only few days turned into twelve long and depressing years.

Then one day she heard that Jesus was passing her way, and suddenly she saw her deliverance. What do you do when you have been down in your mess so long and have lost all hope of ever getting out, and one day you see a glimmer of hope?

This woman did the unexpected...

The woman saw her deliverance passing by and said, 'If I may but just touch the hem of his garment, I shall be made whole.' She was not hoping to meet Jesus face to face, as she knew the consequence of even being in the crowd; all she wanted was a touch. Not for Jesus to lay his hand on her and rebuke her infirmities, not for Jesus to encourage or hold her; but all she wanted was to touch the smallest part of Jesus' garment. Her touch mixed with her faith ended her twelve years of embarrassment and suffering. She was made whole.

Do you want to be made whole?

Many times in life we are thrown in a situation or environment that seems contrary, an environment that sinks us in depression that sucks every substance or breath out of our bodies. You know you're sick and that to get your healing you have to get up in the midst of church service and shout. How do you do that when everyone already sees you as nothing, and what you're about to do is contrary to the normal way of doing things? You are the one dying inside and each day has to go home and face your situation, all alone. What do you do?

More importantly, what do you want in life? Where should you have been right now if you had stepped out and done the unexpected when the opportunity came? Life expects you to behave in a certain manner and everyone is looking at you and saying this is who you are, and this is what I expect of you, even if their expectation is suffocating the very essence of life out of you. You're in an environment and you want to express yourself in a certain manner, but if you do you'll face the wrath of those around you. What do you do?

What do you do when life gives you lemons and you're expected to play your part, holding onto the lemon instead of making lemonade? This is the dilemma the woman with the issue of blood faced; and this is why when Jesus asked who touched him, she was afraid to reveal her identity.

What do you do when you are surrounded by a wall of flesh that's suffocating you? When there are layers of flesh that seek to stop your growth, healing, purpose and deliverance?

There are many people at this present moment that are not fulfilling their purpose, people that are stuck at one level of their lives because they are afraid to step out and be noticed; afraid of stepping out of the box they locked themselves in; afraid of what people might say or do. They have become so accustomed to the negative words and perceptions of people that they have become experts on what people will say or do days in advance, and thus become their own worst enemy. Immediately, without waiting for people to object, they start giving excuses of what they can and cannot do and why they cannot do it; excuses that not even God knew about. Therefore they become so weighed down with inferiority, thoughts of being a failure, and low self-esteem that their gifts starts to die slowly, and then slowly they become stagnant. Continually, they go around in the wilderness when they should have been in the Promise Land, forever asking God to take them out of their wilderness, not realizing that they are there because of their own thoughts.

There was a time when all the negative words were coming from people around them; but now they are coming from their inner self. 'I can't do this, I am a nobody, I will never be more than what people says I am, I am nothing good,' and the list goes on. Their thoughts of inferiority and low self-esteem start to affect how they behave. All around them their perception of self are reinforced by the negative words of others: 'You see what I was telling you, that he was nothing good.' They feel out of place and like they do not belong anywhere.

What do you do when you face two Great Walls standing before you: yourself and the people around you?

I tell you what you do: you shout your wall down and push through the rubble. To get anything from God and to be whom He says you are, and in order to grow you must be willing to do the unexpected. You must be willing to step out by faith and mentally (or physically, depending on your situation) say goodbye to yourself and those around you. You must be willing to change your perception of yourself, and your circumstances. Your circumstances don't make you, your thoughts do; it is how you perceive life, yourself, and things around you. You have two choices to make: either you're going to allow the environment and circumstances you're in to hold you back, or you're going to be like the woman with the issue of blood who decided that today was her day of deliverance. The choice is yours.

Do you want to be whole? I am not asking you if you want a job to feel complete, to get married so you can feel happy, or to have money in your pocket; I am not asking you if you want material blessings or if you want God to remove all the negative people out of your life. I am asking if you want to get up out of your bed of low self-esteem, depression, hopelessness, a life with no meaning and failure, to be who God created you to be. Do you want to live a fulfilled life? Do you want to live an empowered life?

Moving Forward

As you go through this day and face the rest of your life, I want you to think about the things that are holding you back. What is the thing or things that are very personal and depressing, that is causing an issue in your life? Perhaps it is preventing you from walking in your purpose or perhaps it is hindering you from being productive at work. Perhaps that thing is holding your marriage in captivity? Perhaps you have been a slave to yourself, or alcoholism, and intoxicated with fear. Whatever your 'issue of blood' may be, it's time to shout your wall down and push through the rubble lying before you. Shouting your wall down may not be physically shouting, but it may be deciding that you will no longer be a slave to yourself, your situation, and the people around you. Mary had to go through a wall of Jesus' disciples slandering her, belittling her and the ugly stares of his disciples and her own fears of touching the master to anoint Jesus (Mark 14:1-9).

Shout until your Jericho wall falls down flat. See you again tomorrow.

Day 26
Learn to Deal with Oppositions

"For you to become a mature individual and for God to use you to do great things, you must first learn how to deal with oppositions. Oppositions at times will come from persons you least expect them from. Will you melt under oppositions, or will you stand?"

Scriptures of the Day: Mark 3:21; Acts 4: 1-22

Discourse

If you should do a survey of all the people who are striving in their career, ministry and are living happy and productive lives, you would learn that all these people learnt how to deal with opposition. They are not afraid of or tremble when even their best friends oppose their ideas or plans; more importantly, they do not hold a grudge. They understand that not everyone will agree with their point of view and not everyone will like them. They have decided that, even when someone opposes them to their face, they will not hold any grudge against that person, nor will they allow opposition to cause them not to grow to their full potential.

Opposition is a part of life and we all have to deal with it. How you deal with it is dependent on how you view life, others, and yourself, how confident you are and your level of maturity. Throughout Jesus' ministry, he faced enormous opposition by the religious and political leaders of his time such as the Pharisees, Sadducees, and Scribes.

On top of all these, he faced opposition and misunderstanding from people that were very close and most dear to him: his family and friends. The Bible tells us:

"And when his friends heard of it, they went out to lay hold on him: for they said, He is beside himself" (Mark 3:21).

What they were basically saying is that Jesus was going crazy, he was out of his mind and they wanted to stop him.

How many times has God given you a vision, directing your life or career down a certain path, or using you in ministry, and those around you who you had expected to give you a listening ear, to help you fulfill God's purpose for your life, are not there for you? Instead of them holding your hands, they are the ones pulling you down, saying all manner of evil against you and wanting to stop you, 'he is beside himself.' What are you going to do when people oppose you?

When Jesus cast out demons and healed the sick, the Scribes who should have been his friends said that, "He hath Beelzebub, and by the prince of the devils casteth he out devils" (Mark 3:22; see also Luke 11: 14-20). When he healed a woman in the synagogue on the Sabbath that had an infirmity for eighteen years, and was bent completely forward so that she could not lift herself up, you would have thought that the ruler of the synagogue, and others in the synagogue, would have been jumping for joy, but instead he was filled with anger and indignation, because Jesus delivered the woman that was bond for eighteen long and painful years (Luke 13: 10-17).

Because Jesus was not on their side, he was a walking target; it was either their way or death. Does that sound familiar to you?

Life can be compared to running a hurdle. The hurdles are there to trip the athlete over so that he or she will fall and discontinue the race. How do you deal with these hurdles? How do you deal with opposition? Here is how:

1. Realize that opposition is a part of life.

2. Listen. You cannot confront opposition unless you first listen and try to understand what they are saying, their intentions and what their plans are.

3. Understand that you are not always right. There is something to be learnt from every negative experience you had. Use your opponents to grow and be better.

4. Hold no grudge against anyone, no matter how much they have hurt you. Jesus laid down his life even for those who were against him.

5. Do not allow anyone to make you feel less than who God calls you to be; nor should you let anyone stop or hinder you from growing as an individual in your career, education, or as a minister of God. At times, you may feel like you're not called by God, you do not deserve to be where you are or what God has given you, that you are not important or you cannot accomplish anything. Do not listen to the lies the enemy speaks in your ears, but reject them forcibly.

6. Do not try to fight your own battles, but let God do the fighting. Fighting our own battles at times can cause the situation to get out of hand, and we ending up losing everything, including the respect and trust of others.

Moving Forward

As you go through this day and look forward to your future, remember that God did not call you to be stagnant or to bow to the demands of the enemy. Each one of us is a warrior and warriors face their opponents, and they do not accept defeat from the enemy. It is the plan of the enemy to destroy that seed, vision or purpose which God has placed in you before it starts bearing fruits. You will forever remain at the same level in life unless you first learn to overcome opposition, and learn from each experience while at the same time you can shake your opponent's hand after if need be without any feeling of hatred, or holding any grudge.

Day 27
Divinely Orchestrated Trials

"It was through pain, trial and persecution that the gospel of Jesus was spread over the known world. The disciples were getting comfortable teaching only in Jerusalem, so God had to use persecution to move them."

Scriptures of the Day: Acts 8: 1-8; 9:1-19

Discourse

Sometimes in your life everything may be going fine and you're doing all that the Lord requires of you, then suddenly, persecutions and trials arise in your life; even your own family turn against you. At this point in your life you may ask, 'God, I have been serving you faithfully, so what is happening in my life? Lord, did I do something wrong? How did my life get to this point? It may seem as if everything happening, you're the architect of it; but I am here to tell you that despite of all you're going through, do not worry, but rejoice. God is using your persecution to usher you into your purpose.

At times God will allow persecution, hardship, trials and many sorrows to come into your personal life and ministry so that He can redirect your focus somewhere else. Sometimes we may get very comfortable in our walk with the Lord, or in any other areas of our lives, and think we are where we should be, probably ignoring that still small voice directing us in a certain path. So the Lord will at times uproot us from our comfort zone so that He can take us on the path we may not have been thinking of walking on. Even though the Lord had commanded His apostles to go throughout the world preaching the gospel, they became comfortable preaching the gospel only at Jerusalem, therefore the Lord had to send persecution to uproot them and send them to other parts of the world to do His work.

What you may be facing now is not by chance; God may want to direct your life in another direction so that you may not be able to see in the state you were in. The prophet Elijah had new revelations and a ministry direction after he ran for his life from Queen Jezebel- it was then he anointed Elisha to take his place and to help him through his ministry. Additionally, it was also at that moment in his ministry he learnt that God was speaking to his rebellious people in a still small voice, not in signs of miracles and wonders of earthquakes, etc. Mighty men were placed in David's life when he was persecuted by Saul, and it was these same men that helped to establish his kingdom and fought his battles. If David did not encounter persecution, then he would not have been able to strengthen the men that came to him while he was at the cave and more importantly, those men would not have helped to establish and keep him alive while he was running from Saul.

What form of persecution is coming your way? What you are facing is not to destroy you, but to:

1. Give you new directions and revelations

2. Make you stronger

3. Draw you closer to God

Moving Forward

God will never give you more than you can bear. "Wherefore lift up the hands which hang down, and the feeble knees" (Hebrews 12:12), and run this race with patience knowing that what you are facing is for a reason and God will never leave you or forsake you throughout all your distress. Allow God to use whatever He sees fit so that He may get the glory out of you and shape you into the man or woman He wants you to be. Everything good costs something. Gold is the most expensive item because it was made in the depth of the fire; so too will God try us in the fire of persecution, so that we may be more precious than gold.

Part 4

The Rise of the Warrior

Day 28
Spend Your Time Wisely

"Every second of your day is very precious. Do not occupy it with things and people that will not add value to your day, but spend it making a difference in your life or in the life of someone else."

Scriptures of the Day: John 9: 1-7; Philippians 4:8-9; Ephesians 5:15-17

Discourse

There is a saying that says, 'Time waits on no man.' That is a true statement, as time does not stop to accommodate any one of us regardless of our socioeconomic background; time is its own boss. It is therefore true that time cannot be managed; since you are not able to manage time, you should try to manage yourself in time. Let me explain: if time keeps on moving and is not controlled by what you do at a particular moment in time, how can you then manage time? You can, however, manage what you do in time.

Each one of us was born in time and exists in time; the fact that you are alive means you are alive for a purpose. Too many of us spend most of our time doing nothing of importance; we walk this earth like our life doesn't mean anything, and thus do nothing with our time. Each day you have breath in your body is time given for you to use to make a difference in your life, or to impact your space- your environment, people you come in contact with, the world as a whole, people in cyberspace.

God has given you this moment, not for you to spend it having meaningless conversations, as the Bible says that every idle or careless words you speak, you will be judged for them on the day of judgment (Matthew 12:36); He did not give you time for you not to better your life or to do something with it. When Jesus was upon the earth, he used time to: rest (yes, you must rest and refocus then move on again), preach the Word of God, teach, manifest the kingdom, and yes, have meaningful socialization and relaxation activities and eat. Jesus used his time wisely to make a difference. What are you doing with your time?

Too often, we spend our time doing things that are meaningless and focusing (whether mentally, emotionally or physically) on people who are not going anywhere and do not any intention of walking in their purpose. Similarly, so many times we spend countless hours focusing or being upset about what someone did or said when we should be focusing on the present and future. How many countless hours have we spent doing things that have no value, or having any positive impact on our life? Can you remember the last time you spent hours worrying about something or quarreling about something someone did? Did it add any value to your life? Life is 10% what happens to you, and 90% how you respond; stop being frustrated about things you cannot change, but instead spend your time thinking and doing things that will give God glory, and impact your life or that of someone else. Yes, the sun is hot, but you being stressed about it will not change the weather condition.

We often spend our time trying to fix or control things we were not made to control and end up messing up someone's life, our future, health, relationships or other aspects of our lives. We try to control what people say about us or our spouse, or when things are not going as we think they should we go ahead and want to change it. Stop spending your time trying to control things you are not supposed to control, but control your attitude about the situation.

Each moment you spend is very precious, whether it is at a church service, at work, school, at home with your family, reading your bible or praying to God, and should be spent meaningfully. If you're at church, then dedicate the time to doing the things of God, as time wasted will never return. You have been given this moment, so use it wisely. One decision or movement you make in time can affect your entire future and the lives of others around you, or that you will come in contact with.

Moving Forward

As you go through this day and move forward in time, be fully persuaded in your mind that you will use the time given to you to make a difference in your life, and the lives of those you come in contact with. More importantly, always try to do things that are pleasing to God, as that's the whole purpose of man (Ecclesiastes 12:13). God gives you this moment for you to improve yourself and your relationship with him, to have meaningful interactions and relationships, and to impact your generation and the ones to come. Things will come that you will not be able to control: your child may get sick, your relationship with your spouse gets rocky, you lose your job; you cannot do anything about what happens, but you can change how you react to each situation you may face, and how you will deal with that situation and ones to come. Will you get upset, curse your boss, and get stressed about what happened and what you should or could have done better, or will you start thinking about what you can now do about what has already happen? What you therefore do in time is your responsibility.

Day 29
Don't Let Fear Cripple You

"The man who is bound by fear of failing will never succeed or grow to his full potential, whether in life as a person, or as a Christian, because how can you move forward if you fear making mistakes? If you fear that what God told you to do is not from God, how will you grow? If you fear going forward and letting go of the past, you will forever be stuck in the past. Fear is therefore the enemy of your purpose and the anointing. Fear keeps you in bondage to self."

Scriptures of the Day: 2 Timothy 1:7; Isaiah 37:1-13

Discourse

Fear is one of the most deadly poisons that the enemy uses to cripple humanity. It does not only stop an individual from accomplishing much in life, or growing as an individual; it also robs an individual of his or her anointing and purpose. There are many people living at this very moment in time that have lost potentially good relationships or lucrative financial and business opportunities, and have not grown to their full potential because of fear.

One of the things with fear that makes it so deadly is that it is widespread and very contagious. Go into a room with everyone being afraid and you too will start feeling fear slowly creeping in. Additionally, many times we cannot explain why we are afraid of something, but just because we saw or heard of someone being afraid of something, we too began to express fear of that thing. Fear robs a person of finding new pathways in life; it robs an individual of their inner peace, joy and happiness, and is powerful enough to rob you of your purpose and anointing. Yet, all of us suffered or have experienced some form of fear one time or another in our lives; and many of you reading this book right now are being crippled spiritually and otherwise by fear. No one is exempt; whether you are well educated or not, in the upper-class or lower class, rich or poor; everyone faces something in life that causes them to be fearful. The fear of the unknown is very powerful.

But what, really, is fear? Fear is an emotion that is displayed when there is an expectation of harm or pain, whether emotionally or physically. Fear is characterized by alarm, dread, and disquiet. But the meaning of fear I would like to look at in this book is the acronym FEAR- False Evidence Appearing to be Real. If you should take the time to look at some of the things you had been fearful of in the past week or month, but are not afraid of anymore, you would immediately ask yourself, 'Why was I afraid of this thing again?' That is why fear is False Evidence Appearing to be Real; it's in our imagination. Yes, we will encounter serious threats in our lives, for example, being attacked by a madman with a gun is nothing to be looked at as being false; it is a real fear that can make a grown man wet his pants. However, the fear I am talking about is the fear of the unknown. The fear of expressing yourself around others; the fear of letting go of the past or someone you really care about; the fear of applying for that job or leaving your family behind to go overseas to further your education; the fear of when the Lord tells you to do something and you immediately freeze because you are afraid of what people may say or do. I am talking about the fear that gets you trembling, but at the same time is not life threatening or really there.

Many of us can testify that fear is one of our biggest problems that we are trying to get rid of; but at the same time we make no real effort to shed ourselves of this deadly skin. I have had times in my life when I should have stood up for my right or the rights of others; but instead of doing what I was supposed to do, I was paralyzed by fear; the consequences sometimes were very costly, emotionally and otherwise. Additionally, there are times when the Lord had specifically told me to pray for someone, but I didn't, and the consequence of not doing so was very costly. A friend of mine was instructed by the Lord to call someone, but she didn't because of fear. The person committed suicide that same night. No wonder the apostle Paul wrote to encourage Timothy not to be fearful when he said, "For God hath not given us the spirit of fear; but of power, and of love, and of a sound mind" (1 Timothy 1:7). No doubt Paul had first-hand experiences of the paralyzing effect fear has on an individual.

There is a great truth I want to share with each one of you, and that is: Fear is only in our imagination; it is not real.

Just because you had a bad experience with someone last week, it doesn't mean you will have the same bad experience with that person the next time around. You called to a gentleman yesterday and he responded in a very harsh manner, but that doesn't mean he will not respond to you in a positive manner the next time around; perhaps he was having a very frustrating morning and you called to him when he was in a very bad state of mind.

I will not lie to you; to get rid of fear will cost you every ounce of strength you have. For example, to stand up to your brother who is always belittling you, or to move out on faith when all your previous experiences were negative; however, once you step out with the knowledge that what you are about to do is the right move, and that God is directing your steps, the reward you will receive could change your life forever. Let go and let God have his way in your life. You will never move forward in life if you allow fear to hold you down. God did not give you the spirit of fear, so fear is therefore not from God, but from the devil- and we know that nothing good comes from the devil, as he only comes "to steal, and to kill, and to destroy. Jesus comes so that you "might have life, and that they might have it more abundantly" (John 10:10). Boldness brings life.

Moving Forward

Many people remain stagnant spiritually and in life because of fear, while they watch others passing them by the roadside- you probably are one of them. Haven't you had enough of fear holding you down?

Perhaps it is time you look in the mirror and ask yourself, 'How long am I going to allow fear to keep me down?' Now rise up against fear by going outside and shout as if you are shouting to someone, and say at the top of your voice: 'I WILL NOT BE AFRAID ANYMORE!!!' Keep repeating it a few times until it's buried in your spirit; say it with confidence. Now whenever fear creeps in, tell yourself, 'I am not afraid, I am not afraid, I am not afraid.' Remember, there will be times you will make mistakes, but do not allow your mistakes to hinder you the next time opportunities come your way, as the only person who never makes a mistake is God. Also remember that the person you are fearful of is a mere human being who also has fears, and is just as much flesh and blood as you are.

Day 30
No Weapon Formed Against You Shall Prosper

"Weapons of mass destruction will rise against you, but if you stand none shall prosper, for no weapon (tongue, demonic attacks, pressures, etc.) that rises against you shall prosper. You will feel the effects of it, but the intention of the enemy shall not come to pass. Sometimes you will feel like bowing under the pressures, as you think the pressures of life are too much for you to bear, but before you do, remember you have a high priest who you can cry to for help, and his love for you dictates that he comes to your rescue."

Scriptures of the Day: Isaiah 46:3-4; 53:14-17

Discourse

So many times the enemy sends darts of deception our way- you will come to nothing good in life; you are a loser; you are weak; you don't deserve to be loved and no one will ever love you; you are a failure, so why don't you just kill yourself; you cannot do this or that; no one will ever listen to your dream; your dream will die- darts of low self-esteem and depression, darts of accusation- who do you think you are? You are a child molester and will never change; you are a prostitute who sells your body for money; darts of people looking down on you and belittling you. On top of all this, the enemy will send arsenals of troubles and misfortune your way so that you either start believing his lies and thus he creates a stronghold in your life, or you start sinking in depression. It is the plan of the enemy to destroy your gift, your purpose, the word that God gave you, your ministry, your family, and your future (John 10:10).

The enemy is a ruthless assassin and thus will use your job, wife or husband, children, best friend, family, friends, church members, circumstances you face each day, the man you see every day at the corner, the media etc. to defeat you. However, the God you and I serve knew before the foundation of the earth the plans of the enemy towards you, and has thus given you some powerful weapons to fight with. "For the weapons of our warfare are not carnal, but mighty through God to the pulling down of strong holds" (2 Corinthians 10:4).

The battle we fight is not a carnal or natural one, though its manifestation is in the physical; it is a spiritual battle, and therefore is not one that we can fight using man's wisdom, fighting against our neighbors, being quarrelsome, etc. The Bible says that greater is in us than is in the world, and he that is with us will fight our battles because the battle is not ours, but the Lord's; we therefore have to use spiritual weapons such as prayer, worship and praise (2 Chronicles 20:21-24; Acts 16:25-26), the Word of God, which is both a defensive and offensive weapon (Ephesian 6:14,17), the name of Jesus, and faith, which is our shield against the attacks of the enemy (Ephesians 6:16).

God did not create us to bow to the pressures of the enemy or to turn our backs on him; but we are to at all times face the enemy head-on. In warfare, whenever you're fighting and turn your back to the enemy, that is when the enemy will have the advantage over you, as you will not be able to see the attack of the enemy.

Yes there will be times when we will feel the pressure of the attack of the enemy, we may even at times be bruised, but "no weapon that is formed against thee shall prosper... This is the heritage of the servants of the Lord..." (Isaiah 53:17). You will feel the pressure and even become depressed, and feel oppressed as the weapon will form; but the intention of the weapon will not come to pass. Perhaps the enemy has set up your family against you, or caused sickness to rock your body; what the Lord is saying to you today is that if you stand your ground, you shall come out victorious; bruised, but in the right places.

Moving Forward

As you go through this day, I want to encourage you to stand your ground against the attacks of the enemy. You may say the enemy has been attacking your finances, family, physical health, marriage, job, for far too long now; but I would like to tell you the hotter the battle, the sweeter the victory. The enemy would not have been attacking on the level he is now if he did not see purpose in you. The reason why he is attacking at the level he is attacking you and your family is because he sees where God is taking you, and he is determined to stop the move of God, but no weapon... With the weapons that God has given us, we are more than conquerors. He may be attacking you with low self-esteem, depression, emotional issues, or your past; but what does the Word of God say about you, your past and your future? When the enemy whispers negativity in your ears, use the Word of God on him and refute everything he says.

Do not let the enemy think you are a weakling and good for nothing, do not let him deceive you with his lies, but stand up and fight him at all costs.

Day 31
The Promise Shall Not Die

"Sometimes the will or command of God may seem contrary, but if he said it, just obey him. God said unto Abraham that through Isaac, the promise shall come; however, what was contrary is that God told Abraham to kill the promised child. If God made you a promise, even if it seems dead, impossible and like it will never happen, do not allow your faith to waver or be dismayed; God cannot lie, nor will He let you down, even when you are below water. Experiences equal trust."

Scriptures of the Day: Romans 4:18-24; Hebrews 11:1-6, 13, 17-19

Discourse

How many of you have received a prophetic word over your life of what God is about to do in your life, but years later you still haven't seen or received what God had promised? What do you do when the promise of God seems to have died and thus will not come to pass? They are many times prophesies went over my life that I thought would have come to pass in less than one year, base on the promise, but some of them at the writing of this book have still not come to pass. It is sometimes very easy to lose faith when we expect something and we are not seeing it manifested. Sometimes it is not that you're wondering if the promise was from God; that you're sure of, but, what do you do while you're waiting on a sure word from God? There are many times while waiting on the manifestation of the spoken word that my faith starts to waver and I have to go back to the Word of God that the promises of God are sure, and even have to remind God about his promises at times. Many times my friends are the ones who always come at the right moment when I am about to give up with a reminder of the promise.

Maybe Abraham must have wondered if it was actually God that had given him the promise of a child; and maybe his friends may have sought to discourage him at times and thus he felt like giving up on the promise of God. 'Surely it has been 20 years now and my wife Sarah is still barren.'

But that's not what the Bible says in Romans 4:18-21. "Hoping in spite of hopeless circumstances, he believed that he would become "the father of many nations," just as he had been told: "This is how many descendants you will have." He did not weaken in faith when he thought about his own body (which was already as good as dead now that he was about a hundred years old) or about Sarah's inability to have children, nor did he doubt God's promise out of a lack of faith. Instead, he became strong in faith and gave glory to God, being absolutely convinced that God would do what he had promised"

Abraham found himself in an impossible situation, but despite what medical science said and the negative words of others around him that the promise would never come to pass, Abraham held on to the promise of God. When your faith is about to weaken, that is when your past experiences and what you learnt of God will come in very handy; Abraham's knowledge and prior personal experiences of God taught him that God is faithful, and whatever He promised, that is what he will do.

There will be times that it seems like the promise(s) God made you will never come to pass, but can I tell you a secret that I learnt: the longer the promise's delay, the greater it is. If you want to know if a promise God made you will change your life or aspects of your life, then look at how long it takes to come to pass. On top of all that, the more blessed you will be, the greater the attacks from the enemy will be for the promise not to come to pass. Abraham did not just have great faith and keep that faith for many years, he had to fight to maintain his faith so that the enemy would not steal the promise. Therefore, instead of complaining and losing hope, you need to start rejoicing. Moreover, there will be times when the promise will be delayed, as God has to position the right people in your life before he can release the promise. There would have been no Esther as a deliverer if Mordecai wasn't in place. Joseph would not have become the most important man in Egypt if the butler wasn't thrown in prison while he was there. Similarly, if Joseph was not thrown into prison, he would have lived and died in Potiphar's house as a slave, as he would not have been in the position to interpret the Butler's dream. Sometimes the Lord will have to put you in some tight situations and then send the right person(s) along so that what he promised will come to pass. Joseph got the dreams when he was 17 years of age, and the vision did not come to pass until he was around 30 years of age.

Moving Forward

The apostle Peter says to the Christian brethren that were scattered abroad, "The Lord is not slack concerning his promise, as some men count slackness…" (2 Peter 3:9). While your friends or family will make you a promise and then go back on that promise, God will never go back on his promise. If he made you a promise, rest assured that he can bring it to pass. As you go through this day, let us all renew our faith in the promises of God, as he is a God that cannot lie.

Day 32
It Is Time for a Payday

"The Bible says, when a thief is caught he should return 7 times what he stole. The devil is a thief (who is not starving), and God has given us power over the enemy, his demons and over his works. What has the enemy stolen from you or someone close to you? Your time of operating below your privilege is over; get radical and use your authority to command him to restore what he has stolen and to take his hands off you and your family. It is your inheritance."

Scriptures of the day: Proverbs 6:30-31; John 10:10; Luke 10:17-20

Discourse

The Bible says, "Men do not despise a thief, if he steal to satisfy his soul when he is hungry; But if he be found, he shall restore sevenfold; he shall give all the substance of his house" (Proverbs 6:30-31).

The enemy is being described as a thief who comes for three purposes: to kill, steal and to destroy. The good thing is that devil does not steal because he is hungry, but because he comes to kill, steal and destroy. Moreover, everything that we have was given to us by God and is for our enjoyment: our job, family, children, material things, our joy and happiness, ministry and gifts, talents, our hope, aspirations and dreams; therefore, anything the devil has taken from you, he did it illegally, and to do so he had to trespass on your territory.

God has given us power over the works of the enemy and his agents (demons, ministers, and witches, amongst others) to destroy his work, plans and to take back all he has stolen from us or someone else we may know; for this great truth, Jesus came to earth and died so we no longer should live below our privilege. He came so that we may regain the authority we lost in the Garden of Eden and thus destroy the works of the enemy. It is this great truth the enemy does not want you to know or believe, because he knows that if you really know who you are and what you are capable of doing, he, his demons and ministers are in big trouble. That is why you had to go through the pain and suffering you've been through, so that you may know what you are fully capable of doing. That is why they lied and mistreated you, because the enemy does not want you to become who God calls you be; nor does he want you to know what you are fully capable of doing. But he made a mistake, because he touched the wrong person; he troubled a child of God who is destined for greatness. All that you have been through and all that the enemy stole from you, God was using it to make you into a weapon of war. He stole your joy, your mind, peace, job, family, children, your future, gifts, church, and ministry because it is his intention for you to self-destruct and die without walking or fulfilling your purpose. Now you need to rise up and tell him enough is enough, you will not take it anymore; what he did yesterday was the last straw. Now you are a warrior that will not lie still anymore and take anything from the enemy.

For the devil to steal from you is like him committing murder, as he did it to destroy or kill you. Are you going to allow him to get away with it? It's war time and you're not taking any prisoners with you. The Bible says in Proverbs 18:21 that "Death and life are in the power of the tongue: and they that love it shall eat the fruit thereof." Power is in your mouth to change the atmosphere or circumstances that hold you captive. When God created man, he created another being that will open his mouth and speak with authority. Jesus came to give back man that authority we lost in the Garden of Eden.

What has the enemy stolen from you? You have already acknowledged that the enemy has stolen from you, and have taken responsibility for allowing him to trespass in your territory and stolen something he had no right to. "But if he be found, he shall restore sevenfold; he shall give all the substance of his house." Now you need to take authority and open your mouth and command him to restore everything he had stolen SEVENFOLD, not one or twofold, but sevenfold. For all the mess the enemy has brought into your life, you deserve more than what he stole from you; you deserve a payday. This is a divine law established in the spiritual realm, and the enemy knows it. That is why he doesn't want you to know the 'tools' or rights given to you, because he knows he will not be able to do all he pleases with you because you will attack him, not as a defeated person, but as a man or woman with power and authority. If you speak with faith, then heaven will back you and he will have to obey and restore all he has stolen.

Moving Forward

As you go through this day, what has the enemy stolen from you, or your family? Perhaps there is a curse running through your generation that is causing much pain and suffering; if you identify it, you must break it, as he has stolen something precious from you and your family. Are you going to stand by and see the enemy destroy you or your family? Aren't you angry enough to do something about it? Perhaps he stolen your gift, ministry, joy, peace, marriage, or finances; whatever it may be, it is not his and he did not give it to you, so he has no right to it. If the enemy has stolen something from you, then you need to stand in authority and command him to return it sevenfold.

Day 33
Calling All Warriors, It's Time To Take Your Stand

"The Israelites were a foreshadow of us, the church, and were the most powerful nation under the sun, when they obeyed God. Just how powerful were they? Two sons of Jacob went and destroyed an entire city; one of David's mighty men killed over 900 men. The same might they had is now given unto us. The enemy is afraid of us when we believe, because he knows the power we carry when we believe and stand in our authority. Stand, believe, and fight."

Scriptures of the day: Genesis 34; Joshua 23:10

Discourse

The Bible said of the children of Israel that one shall chase a thousand, and two put ten thousand to flight (Joshua 23:10). Even though this provision was made to the Israelites, God is giving each one of us access to this and all the other promises he made to the Children of Israel (2 Corinthians 1:20). Like Gideon, many of us think of ourselves as weaklings and of no importance; the good news is that God does not see us as we see ourselves. God saw Gideon as a mighty warrior, while he saw himself as a weakling; God saw him as a man of great importance, and he saw himself as insignificant and a nobody (Judges 6). When the children of Israel were to go over to Canaan land to conquer the territory, they could not because THEY SAW THEMSELVES as grasshoppers. It was not that the people were tall and saw the Israelites as grasshoppers, but the Israelites saw themselves as grasshoppers.

How do you see yourself? The truth is, it is not how those around you see you that is really important; it is how you see yourself and what God is saying about you. You may think that you are a nobody, a weakling, and you may even think that you will never come to anything good in life; but what is God saying about you?

When God created man and everything else, Genesis looked and "saw every thing that he made, and, behold, it was very good" (Genesis 1:31). He saw man as powerful and able to rule his territory and future. However, many of us have listened to the deception of the enemy, who tells us that we are not mighty men and women, but are grasshoppers. He tells us that we will never come to anything good, when God said everything you need to be great he has already given it you at conception- only to be manifested in its season. God called you for greatness even before you were born. God said unto Jeremiah, "Before I formed you in the womb I knew you, before you were born I set you apart; I appointed you as a prophet to the nations" (Jeremiah 1:4-5).

Greatness is locked up inside of you from before you were born. You did not become great when you got your first job or degree or when you were given some leadership position; you were destined for greatness before you were born. Your appointment was just a manifestation of what was already in the mind of God.

Do not allow the devil or anyone to whisper in your ears that you are not powerful, you are not a warrior and you cannot do anything right. You are who God says you are, and he says you are a victor, not a victim; he says you are strong, not a weakling; he says you shall be great, not that you will live your life below your privilege. You are more than you think you are, not what people may make you think. If you see yourself contrary to how God sees you, it is high time you start seeing through the eyes of your creator, not through the subjective lenses of people who mean you no good.

Moving Forward

As you go through this day, consider how you have been thinking about yourself and challenge that perception. If you say you are a mighty man or woman, then that is exactly what you are. There is an eagle living inside of you; release it as God wants to show you things we've never seen before. There is a lion within you to conquer or rule over the forces of evil, and our destiny as the lion is the king of the jungle. There is something powerful that God has placed within each one of us. It is your responsibility to be who God created you to be; do not listen to all the negatives the enemy is whispering in your ears and tune into what God is saying about you.

Day 34
Don't Be Ruled by Your Past

"Our past failure and or situations oftentimes affect or determine how we will react to our present situation(s) or life. But isn't it time to let the past go? Stop using your past experiences and stop complaining about this and that, but get up and 'launch out into the deep and let down your nets for a draught.'"

Scriptures of the day: Luke 5: 1-11; St. John 21:3-6, 11; Philippians 3:13-14

Discourse

One of Jesus' first disciple, Simon Peter, in the book of Luke 5, is a very good example of most of us today. Peter, and no doubt his partners in the other boat, were fishing for many hours, but caught nothing when Jesus met them. He was frustrated and became doubtful of ever catching any fish. Probably it was this catch he was depending on to take care of him and his family; perhaps he desperately needed some money to take care of his bills and was having a very unfruitful, hopeless and depressing night and day. There comes this carpenter son who probably knew nothing about fishing and his present situation who tells him to go out in the deep and let down his net for a great catch. Peter must have been thinking that this man was crazy; 'Hasn't he noticed I have been here all night until now and have caught nothing?'

However, just to please Jesus, Peter obeyed and did as Jesus commanded. Can you guess what happened when Peter obeyed Jesus' command and went back into the very place he was coming from and let down his net? The Bible says, "And when they had this done, they enclosed a great multitude of fishes: and their net brake" (Luke 5:6).

You may have been trying to do something for a very long time, and everything you tried failed. You look around and your friends are prospering, but you are not. You may have questioned God over and over about why you are facing this dilemma, but God has given you no answer. Your feeling is never understandable, but what is God saying in your situation? God may be saying one of two things:

1. Try again. Peter was able to catch more fish than he ever caught in his whole fishing career when he tried again. God does not promise that He will come when you call Him, but He promise to always be there for you. Your timing is not His timing. The world is operated by seasons, a season of failure and a season of success (Ecclesiastes 3). When it is your season, you will walk in it and forget the all-night toiling. Therefore, be persistent in your pursuits and always try to listen to that still small voice giving you direction. Perhaps the still small voice is saying back down for a season, as your season of prosperity or success is not yet.

2. Try something else. The fact is that everyone wasn't born to be a fisherman, policeman, pastor, doctor, educator, etc. but everyone was born for a purpose. Each person was given a key to unlock a door that only you can. Yes, there will be other doctors, but no one else can practice medicine like you. There may be other educators, but no else can teach like you. Sometimes we are holding on to things that we should not, and because of that, we continue down a road of torment, failures and disappointments. There is a time to start something, and there is also a time to quit.

The signs will be there of what God wants you to do; follow them.

Moving Forward

Do not allow your past to continually hinder your progress. You may have tried many times to bake a cake, but kept failing and simply gave up. What if you should try again and develop a recipe that will make you a millionaire? You will never grow further than your past if you continually allow your past to hinder your future. Throw every rubbish of your past in a garbage truck, or garbage bin, and look no longer for it; nor should you consider it, "for the former things are passed away," and behold God makes all things new (Revelation 21:4-5).

Day 35
Don't Put Your Weapons Down

"Our spiritual battles are not won with swords, arguments, or weapons of this world, but they are won with spiritual weapons and faith given to us by God."

Scriptures of the day: 2 Corinthians 10:3-5; Ephesians 6:10-18

Discourse

The bible declares in 2 Corinthians 10:3-5 and Ephesians 6 that we are fighting a spiritual war every day. It is not a war against your neighbor, family, workplace, the man on the street, etc., (although the enemy will use them as his tool to fight against you), but the battle is waged in the spiritual realm and its manifestations are seen in the earthly realm. The physical realm affects the spiritual realm, and the spiritual realm affects the physical- both are interwoven and thus inseparable. It's a war that each one of us have to fight; no one is excluded, as each one of us is plunged into a war that wasn't started by us, but still we have to fight from we came out of our mother's womb.

Oftentimes because we are not seeing what is happening in the spiritual realm, when for example our neighbor starts arguing with us for no apparent reason, or everything in our life seems to turn upside down, we quickly start using carnality (quarreling, anger and wrath, wisdom and other things of this world) to fight back, resulting in us losing the battle. Simply put, you cannot use physical things to fight a spiritual war. The Word of God declares, "For though we walk in the flesh, we do not war after the flesh: (For the weapons of our warfare are not carnal, but mighty through God to the pulling down of strong holds;) (2

Corinthians 10: 3-4).

The Bible describes the devil as very subtle (Genesis 3:1), meaning that he will attack you very skillfully, oftentimes disguising himself. That is why the apostle Paul was encouraging the Ephesians brethren in Ephesians 6:11 that they should "Put on the whole armour of God, that ye may be able to stand against the wiles of the devil." Wiles speak of the devil as being very crafty or cunning, always trying to hide what he is doing; for example, attacking you with sickness so that you will not fight back, attacking your finances, using everyday situations to fight you. Many people think that the enemy will come and attack them in his true colors, or only attack us through very devious means such as witchcraft and other means, but the enemy does not always like to be seen; he does his greatest work under cover.

The enemy attacks us using three main weapons: Deception, Temptations and Accusations.

Deception

Deception is basically making you believe a lie. It sometimes involves twisting the Word of God or mixing a truth with a lie; for example, when he attacked Eve in the Garden of Eden and caused Eve to doubt the Word of God and then injected his own ideology into the mind of Eve- he used the Word of God and then added a lie.

Examples of deception the devil will use on you are: you're worthless and will never come to anything good in life, God cannot heal you of cancer, you're a nobody and do not deserve to be loved, or you're weak amongst others. That's the same weapon the enemy used on Gideon to let him belittle himself, and is the same weapon he is using today in the churches, media, schools and in our daily lives.

Temptations

A temptation normally follows a deception. For example, nothing is wrong with having sex, it's just harmless fun and if God did not want you to have sex he would not have given you these feelings. Eve started seeing the fruit as pleasing and thus started eating it after the enemy deceived her. Temptations are everywhere, and the enemy plays on our desires to destroy us. Sin is like a bull dog; the more you feed it, the more it will grow. The enemy will show you the worm, but not the hook behind it.

Accusation

The enemy will use your past to haunt you by reminding you of what you did or who you were. It is therefore important that you remind the enemy that God has forgiven you and you are no more what he says you are. Do not listen or entertain the thoughts of the enemy.

The enemy will use these three, more so the weapons of deception and accusation to build strongholds. Strongholds are deceptive thoughts or a way of thinking that controls an individual, community or country. These thoughts can then form the culture of a set of people or family. Strongholds then lead to curses in a community or family (generational curse). Two examples are:

1. The enemy may deceive a member of a family, for example the father, to start gambling for various reasons. The father then becomes hooked on gambling and this follows in the family for generations to come.

2. Many people, especially Jamaicans, oftentimes when they have a child would plant the child's navel string under a papaya tree; this is bringing a curse on the child. Similarly, many people when they have building projects would throw alcohol on the ground, saying they are feeding spirits; this again is bringing a curse on the land and anyone who lives on the land will come under the curse unless it's broken, even after 100 years.

It is therefore important for us to know the tricks and or tactics of the enemy and use the weapons God gave us against him. These weapons can be: praying, praise and worship, the name of Jesus, the blood of Jesus and the Word of God.

Moving Forward

As you go through this day, consider what weapon the enemy may be using to attack you or someone you love. You have the power to break any generational curse out of your family and life through prayer and sometimes fasting. Whether you want to believe it or not, you are fighting spiritual warfare every day. God has given us power over the works of the enemy; it is for us to use all that He has given us to fight an unseen foe.

Part 5
Your Relationship with God

Day 36
Don't Let Go of Faith

"Like the umbilical cord is attached from the baby to the mother, so are we connected to our source, which is God. It is only that our umbilical cord is our faith. Never let your cord get disconnected; it's all we have and it's what we use to draw all that we need from God."

Scripture of the Day: Hebrews 11: 1-2, 6; Romans 4: 18-21

Discourse

Our faith can be likened to that of an umbilical cord, the purpose of which is to give nourishment to the unborn child while it's in the mother's womb. Everything the child needs to stay alive is given to that child through the umbilical cord, which is attached from the mother to the child. If the umbilical cord should get cut, then the child will not survive while in the mother's womb.

Likewise, if we should lose our faith in God, then we will fail to be who God created us to be; nor will we live a life of true peace, joy and happiness. The spiritual realm is activated by faith; in other words, for anything to be done, it must be done through faith- even the angels and demons work through faith. That is why the enemy always attacks our fundamental faith, because if the foundation is weak, then everything at the top will crumble. There are many times when I am going through some crisis in my life and it seems as if God is not there, and in order to be an overcomer I had to lean on my previous experiences with God and all I knew already knew about Him. If our faith should crumble, we would live a very miserable life.

Our faith in God is the reason why we can go to bed with the assurance that He will protect us, why we can leave our life in His hands each day we step out on the road; if our faith is ever broken, then all hell could break lose in our mind and life. Many people live reckless lives because they fail to believe that God could ever love or care about them.

There are many people living in the world right now who are living a sinful life, not because they want to, but because they believe that they have drifted so far from God that God can never forgive and or love them. This therefore has caused many to live reckless lives. At the same time, many people have looked over their life of heartaches and suffering and thought God would never allow those things to happen to them if He loves them. Their spiritual umbilical cord- which is their faith in God and His love- has been cut. Faith releases us from torment.

Many times we cannot understand why God does some things at times; for example, why He allowed your mom to die, or why He allowed your only child to die or to be in and out of the hospital, if He is a loving God. We will never at times understand why the Lord does some things; however, we can rest assured that He loves each one of with unfailing love, regardless of who we are, or what we may have done in our past. His love for us is unchanging. God does things for His own divine purpose, a purpose we may not see or understand while we are in the process. I have learnt that just because God did not stop certain things from happening or intervene, it does not mean that He was not there when it happened, or He doesn't love you. He sometimes does things because He knows that the experience you've been through or are currently facing will not break you, but will make you stronger- and if it breaks you, He will build you back up again.

The enemy comes to steal, kill and destroy (John 10:10), and one method he uses to destroy humanity is to attack their faith, because when you take away a man's faith, you take away hope and give him despair; take away his purpose and his life will be meaningless; take away his faith in God and you will take away his joy, happiness, and peace; you take away everything he needs to survive.

Faith is standing on the word or promises of God, even when it seems like God is not there or will not come through for you. Faith is knowing that no matter what you have done throughout your life and will do,

God still loves you. Faith is knowing that He is your protector, provider, healer, and way-maker, even when what you are seeing is contrary to the fact. Faith is standing even when you feel like throwing in the towel, because you know that, despite what is going on, He is still a good God, and all things work together for good to them that love God and are called according to His divine purpose. Faith is believing that whatever He says that He will do, and whatever you ask in faith, believing He will grant it according to HIS divine will and purpose. Faith will let you raise the dead, heal the sick, overcome poverty and become a millionaire; through faith you can do all things.

Moving Forward

As you go through this day, I want to encourage you not lose your faith in God. Situations will come that will test your faith, but remember God says He will never leave you, nor forsake you. Every promise God made to people and His servants in the bible is still available to each one of us today, and whatever He did back then, He can still do it today.

"Your word, LORD, is eternal; it stands firm in the heavens" (Psalms 119: 89, NIV).

"The very essence of your words is truth; all your just regulations will stand forever" (Psalms 119: 160).

Day 37
Be Persistent in Prayer

"Like the widow who persistently pleads her case to the unjust judge for justice, in the same manner the Lord wants us to persistently call upon Him through prayer and fasting until He answers."

Scriptures of the Day: Luke 18:1-8; Philippians 4:6-8

Discourse

Many people ask the question, 'If the Lord knows everything, and He hears our prayers the first time we pray, why does He sometimes have us praying for days, weeks or even years about something before He answers? Why do we actually need to pray to Him if He knows before we ask what we need?' These are some of the questions asked not only by non-Christians, but also by many Christians. I will not pretend I know all the answers to these questions, but based on biblical principles and experiences, I have come to understand that there are several reasons for this:

1. Many of us would stop seeking the Lord in prayer if He should grant our request the first time we ask. We understand from the account in Genesis 3:8 that God would come down in the cool of the day and talk with His creation each day. God is a speaking God, and when He created man, He created man to have an intimate relationship with him; not to act as a 'sugar daddy'. If we should be honest with ourselves, the main reason why some of us pray often and are such great prayer warriors is because we had to spend many hours on our knees before God granted our request. The Lord does not promise that He will answer our prayers immediately when we ask, but He promises that He will answer; at times He will answer immediately, and at other times He will answer after a period of time as He said in His Word: "Ask, and it shall be given you; seek, and ye shall find; knock, and it shall be opened unto you: For every one that asketh receiveth; and he that seeketh findeth; and to

him that knocketh it shall be opened" (Matthew 7:7-8).

The Lord knows that the day He grants some of us our requests is the day we stop praying. He therefore sometimes holds out on our blessings until we want the 'blesser' (Him, God) more than the blessing; the 'blesser' and not the benefits. Many of us come to God because we see Him as a World Bank where we can go and make a withdrawal whenever we want without ever making a deposit; a magician who will wield his wand and make all our problems go away. God never promises that He will be your butler, your banker or your assistant who you call upon when you need something, then dismiss Him when He finishes the job you called Him to do. He therefore sometimes has to delay our request until we learn to appreciate Him for more than what He can give us.

2. We are not ready for what we asked Him. The children of Israel remind us of a people who constantly begged God for a king when God was not ready to give them a king; as a result, they ended up getting a king that wasn't fit for the position (1 King 8). How many times have we asked for things only to realize that we weren't ready for it? As our loving Father who knows us more than we know ourselves, it is not His will to give us anything that we're not ready to receive as yet; that is why many times we have to wait years before He blesses us with a ministry, car, house, money and other material or spiritual things. He knows that if He blesses you with that spiritual gift, or job you have been asking for, you will not be able to handle the pressure that comes with it. He knows that if He blesses you with that car and house you have been asking Him for, you will be lifted up in pride. He knows that if He blesses you with wealth, you will put the blessing over the 'blesser'. He therefore at times withholds what He has in store for us until we are at the place emotionally, spiritual and/or otherwise, before He releases the blessing or the promise.

Sometimes in order for God to bless or give you what He has in store for you, like a master chest player He has to move around some things and set up some people before He can release your blessing.

3. Sometimes our prayers and answers are being blocked by high level demons and witches in the second heaven. The bible told us of a man by the name of Daniel. Daniel wanted some answers from God about his people, the children of Israel, who were held captive as slaves in Babylon, so he went to God for answers. The bible let us know that the same minute Daniel opened his mouth to God, the answer was sent by an angel, but Daniel did not get the answers until 21 days later. Why? Daniel did not receive the answers because the angel God sent to give him the answers were hindered by a prince demon who controlled the territory (Daniel 9:20-27).

When we enter into prayer, we enter into a war zone where there are high level demons and witches assigned to block us when we pray from receiving the answer from God. Daniel had to fast for 21 days before the angel could get release from the prince demon holding him captive. Prayer is not only about opening our mouth and saying a few words; sometimes we will have to enter into spiritual warfare, where we pull down strongholds and break the powers of Satan that are stopping our breakthrough. Ensure that you have on the whole armor of God, as any part of you that is uncovered by the armor, that's the same area that will be unprotected by your angel. If your angel is under attack, then you also are under attack.

4. Our motives are wrong. It is God's will to give us our hearts desire, however, if our motives for asking something are wrong, then He will not grant it. If you are asking Him for a car so that you can boast on your friends, then He will not give you a car. Before you start asking, ensure that your motives are pure (James 4:2-3).

5. It is not aligning with the will or Word of God. Many times we ask God for things that are not really bad, but are just not in the will or plan of God for our life. That is why sometimes we need to be careful of the things we ask for and listen to the voice of God when He says no. Many times the Lord is taking us in another direction, but because we are stubborn and set in our own ways we keep asking Him for something He already said no to. There are two main wills of the Lord: the permissive

will and the divine will. The permissive will is what He gives us because we keep asking Him for it when He is not ready to give us, or it's not in His will for our lives; and His divine will is His will for our lives. When we keep asking Him for things that are not in His will we end up in trouble, like the children of Israel when they asked for a king.

Moving Forward

As you go through the day, take a moment to ponder what is it you are asking the Lord for and why. It is the will of God to answer our prayers, however, we need to ensure that our prayers are sincere and according to His will. God loves to listen and talk with His creation, as when He created man, He created man to have a relationship with him. God wants to talk to you, and He wants you to talk to Him, but you first need to make the first step.

Day 38
Wait on the Lord's Timing

"The Lord sometimes will not heal or take you out of crisis, but like Lazarus, will allow you to die so that He may raise you up again and show His power through your death and resurrection."

Scripture of the Day: St. John 11:1-44

Discourse

Many times we find ourselves in a very impossible situation and expect the Lord to show up and immediately take us out of it. This was what was happening in the Bible story of Lazarus. Lazarus, whom Jesus loved very much, was sick and near to death; he and his sisters called and expected Jesus to show up immediately on hearing that he was sick, but Jesus chose instead to wait until Lazarus was dead for, not one or two days, but four days; four days when his flesh was supposed to be rotting and starting to give off a foul smell, four days when he knew people would criticize and question his love for Lazarus, four days when there was nothing humanly possible to be done for Lazarus. Many times the Lord will see us struggling and wait until there seems to be no way out of what we may be facing; our situation is dead and we have already started to stink for many days. It is then that you start seeking answers for why God allowed your only child to die when He could have healed him of that sickness; why He allowed your child to be locked up in prison and facing many years of imprisonment; why He allows your situation to get out of hand when He is God of all things.

I am here to tell you that sometimes the Lord will choose you and what you are facing to show forth His love and power to you and those around you. God could have prevented Lazarus from dying, but if He did many people would not have believed Him; and we wouldn't have known from the scriptures that He is a God who can raise the dead. He could have prevented you from being thrown out of college, but instead

He chose to have you being kicked out and criticized by neighbors, family and friends: 'He goes to church every Sunday, where is God his now?' 'If God could let that happen to him, I will never become a Christian.' 'What kind of God would allow his servant to be treated in such a disgraceful manner?'

Mary and Martha could not understand why Jesus did not come when they knew he loved them dearly and could have healed Lazarus of his sickness. They were in tears and cried themselves to sleep night after night. Why? they asked. The loss of their brother was very devastating and heart-breaking, but they never questioned the love and power of Jesus, even when he did not show up in their situation.

What do you do when God seems to turn His back on you? Do you still trust Him? Even when your situation has been dead for many days and has already started to smell? Will you turn your back on Him and say you will never serve or trust Him again? Will you stop praying? Will your heart become cold because He allowed your one son to die by the hands of gunmen? What will you do when you have been praying about a situation for many years and He doesn't answer?

The true test of a man's character and love for God is not when everything is going right in his life; the bills are being paid on time, kids are going to school, money is in the bank, everyone in your household is healthy, your marriage couldn't be better- life is all good. The true test of your character and love for God is when all hell is breaking loose in your life and you can still say, 'Lord, although things are not going right in my life and I feel forsaken, I will still lift my hands and worship you from the bottom of my heart.' The true test of your character and love for God is when all hell is breaking loose in your life and instead of complaining and blaming God, you bow your knees and worship and say like Job, "Naked I came from my mother's womb, and naked I will depart. The LORD gave and the LORD has taken away; may the name of the LORD be praised" (Job 1:21). When your friends and loved ones are telling you to stop going to church and praising God because God has forgotten you, but in spite of your present circumstances, you still maintain your faith in the God that seems to turn His back on you.

Sometimes the Lord will put you through hunger so you will testify that he is a provider, through sorrow so you will know the depth of his love and power, or through afflictions and persecution so you will be strong and mature in your faith.

The question then is, what is God trying to do in my life? What is He trying to do, why does He allow all these troubles to come my way? 'Lord, you said favor is on my life and I'm blessed, but right now I don't feel blessed; I don't feel you right now and you said you will always be there for me.'

Throughout Jesus' ministry he addressed God as his Father; but when he was on the cross, he said, "My God, my God, why hast thou forsaken me" (Matthew 27:46)? Jesus never felt so forsaken and alone until he was on the cross, until he was about to take his work to another level by redeeming mankind. Throughout Jesus' career he felt the Father's love and presence, but at the most critical time of his life the Father was not there. What is Jesus trying to tell us today? He knew that God was there with him and he was loved. He knew the purpose of him coming to earth, so what then is the significance of this statement?

Many revelations and interpretations can be deduced from this one statement, but the one I would like to make known unto you is relevant to our discussion here and that is, whenever God is about to take you to the next level of your life or to reveal himself to you at a deeper level, you will always feel the pinch of Him not being there. You will feel forsaken and feel as if all hell is breaking loose in your life. God is about to do some things in your life that will be so powerful that you will not remember the sleepless nights and afflictions, such as, 1. God is about to take you to another level; 2. God's getting ready to take you into your ministry (or another level of it); 3. God is preparing to reveal Himself to you like He has never done before; 4. God is about to use all you have been through as a message that will deliver or strengthen someone else. God trusted you with trouble.

The Lord allowed Lazarus to die because He knew He would raise him up again, and by His miracle many would believe in Him. It was through the resurrection of Lazarus we can preach and encourage others that even when He is four days late, He is still an on time God. How can Jesus be four days late for your situation, but still be on time? How can He be on time to get your son out of prison when the case has been tried and your son is behind bars? When you're in the hospital and the doctors says you will not live to see the next morning? He is on time for your situation, because there is no situation that is too big for Him to handle, even when it seems too late. I know you have probably heard this already, but I want to encourage you that in whatever situation you find yourself in, God is able to deliver you, and if He does not deliver you, God is saying that I am sending trouble your way to test your character and make you more fruitful.

Moving Forward

What situations are you going through right now that seem hopeless? As you go through this day, I want you to think of the story of Lazarus and how the Lord waited until he was dead for four days to show up. God never promises any of us that He will show up in our time or when we want Him to, but He promises He will always be there for you.

Day 39
God Is Calling You to Another Level

"It is the will of God for you to always move forward and not backward. When the Israelites were coming out of Egypt and going into the Promise Land, the Egyptian army was behind them wanting to take them back into slavery, while the Red Sea was before them. Going back into slavery was not an option; they only had one choice, and that was to go forward."

Scriptures of the Day: Isaiah 43: 18-19; Jeremiah 29:11; Job 17:9

Discourse

There will be times in your life when your past will try to catch up with you with the intention of dragging you back into the mess you are coming out of. Not only that, when you look ahead of you all you see is road blocks, and you may think that there is no way out of your situation. With no apparent way out of your dilemma, it may seem like the best option you have is to go back to your former state (for example, drug abuse, crime and violence, sexual promiscuity, and the list goes on) as you may think the road ahead is too difficult for you to cross.

If you are in this position right now, I encourage you not to go back from where the Lord has taken you from; do not go back into Egypt. Egypt represents the sin, disgrace and hardship that God has taken you out of. When the Children of Israel were coming out of Egypt from over 400 years of disgrace in slavery, their past (the Egyptians) sought to bring them back to where they were coming from. There came a time in their journey that the Egyptian army was closing in on them, and before them was the Red Sea. They were trapped and running out of options. They were not warriors, so they did not know how to fight, and they could not all swim across the Red Sea. What were they going to do? Some contemplated going into the Red Sea, as they would rather drown in the Red Sea than to be taken back into slavery; some perhaps thought about stoning Moses, for he was the one God had used to deliver them from out of Egypt, while some thought of surrendering to the Egyptians.

This was when Moses "said unto the people, Fear ye not, stand still, and see the salvation of the Lord, which he will shew to you today: for the Egyptians whom ye have seen today, ye shall see them again no more forever. The Lord shall fight for you, and ye shall hold your peace" (Exodus 14:13-14).

What is it you have come out of that seeks to bring you back into captivity? Perhaps your Egyptian is a failed relationship, drug abuse, crime and violence, a life of promiscuity, or reveling. Whatever your past is, God wants you to go forward and not backward; do not go back to what you left behind. He did not bring you out of the mess you were in for you to go back in it. Perhaps you may be at your Red Sea right now, and all that is before you is pure water. You see no way out and you may think the only option you now have is to go back to what you're accustomed to; I want to encourage you to continually go forward. If God brought you to a place in your life that all you see before you is an impossible situation, if you stay in faith it is His responsibility to take you through it and into the Promise Land; it is His responsibility to take you to another level of prosperity and blessing in your life. Some of you reading this book, God is getting ready to part your Red Sea so you can walk on dry land. All God is asking you to do is to trust Him and let Him go before you.

It is the plan of the enemy to always let us see the Red Sea before us and Pharaoh's army behind us, but the Word of God will let you see beyond your wilderness or Red Sea experience and see the awesome power of God in operation. The Word of God will let you see the fertile land of Canaan that lies over the Red Sea. God is not slack or unfaithful concerning His promises towards you, and even if you can't see any way out of your situation, the God you serve is capable of making a way even where there seems to be no way. He specializes in doing what seems to be impossible.

Moving Forward

At times it will be difficult for us to overcome the things that we had become accustomed to, and a life of purity of mind, spirit and body may seem very difficult. We may at times think going back to where we are coming from is the best option for us. We may even at times find ourselves slowly going back into Egypt. When this happens, do not to panic; yes, you will slip at times, but God will never condemn or forsake you. Mistakes are a part of growing. God has taken you from a mighty long way and He is not finished with you. He therefore wants you to go forward. God is asking you to: fear not, press on, use what He has given you to destroy the enemy of your past, the enemy blocking your purpose or destiny, which is your faith. Do not let the enticement of your past get a hold of you.

Day 40
What Is Your Motive for Serving God?

"What is your motive for serving God? Are you only serving Him because He can bless you with material things? He will heal you when you're sick? Are you only serving Him because you want to escape hell? Or is it because you have experienced His unfailing love and faithfulness to you and want to serve Him for who He is? What is your reason for serving God?"

Scriptures of the Day: Colossians 3:1-2; Matthew 6:31-33

Discourse

For today's word I want each one of us to take a minute and ponder this question: 'What is my reason for serving God? Do I only worship Him when everything is going right in my life? Am I only worshipping Him because I want a car, house, to get married and so on? What is my true reason for serving God?' I encourage you not to let this day end without being honest with yourself, and with God. The answer to these questions might change your life and perspective forever.

I strongly believe that many of us, if not all of us, came to God for various reasons; not all of us gave our lives to God because of who He is- our savior. Probably you got baptized because someone prophesied danger over your life and the only way to escape was to get covered under the blood of Jesus through baptism, or perhaps you gave your life to God because you heard so many stories about hell and you wanted to escape this horrible fate. Whatever may be your reason for starting on this journey, you're here now, and I am sure by now you might have realized that it's a journey that is both rewarding and difficult.

However, I would like to direct your attention to a fact of life. The fact is

God did not create us so that we may see Him as our 'sugar daddy' who we can call upon whenever we need our bills paid, when sickness is rocking our body, or when we need Him to fix an aspect of our marriage or life. No, God created us to have an intimate relationship with Him. It is His desire for His creation to know Him, and for God and man to communicate together as friends. Yes, I know many of you may think God talking to you is crazy thinking and that doesn't happen anymore; God only talked to the prophets and apostles mentioned in the Bible. I want to tell you right now that if you think God does not talk with His creation like He did with His servants in the Bible, you have being deceived. Let me ask you one question: would you want a father that ONLY listens to you and just fixes issues as they arise in your life? Is that the only role of your father? Or do you want a father who will not only listens to you, but also talk to you? Wouldn't you want an intimate relationship with the one who created you?

God wants us to know Him intimately, and for us to know that His personality and attributes are similar to us. We share traits with our creator because we were created in His image and likeness (Genesis 1:26). Let me ask you one question: if creation shares traits with its creator, and it's man's innate need to form relationships, wouldn't you agree then that need came from God? When you look at any form of creation (cars, gadgets etc.), one thing is common in all, and that is that all created things share traits with its creator.

Not that I am making any accusations, since we are all in agreement with what is said in the previous paragraph, so shouldn't our reason for serving God be to get closer to Him? To develop an intimate relationship with the one who created us, and not for material and or worldly pleasures, or anything that He can give us?

Like many of us today, the Children of Israel did not understand the main reason of their existence, as the Bible says they knew God by His acts (what He could do for them), not His ways (Psalms 103:7). God told the prophet Hosea to go and marry a prostitute woman so as to represent the people of Israel, who at the time were being very unfaithful to God- behaving similarly to a prostitute. In obedience to God's commandment, Hosea went and married Gomer, knowing from the start that she would never be faithful unto him.

Israel was a very prosperous nation, as God had blessed them with material wealth and everything they wanted. When they needed protection from their enemies, God fought and delivered them. When they were sick, God became their healer. When they needed counsel, God sent them counselors. When they needed material things and food, God ensured that their crops always yielded bountifully; Israel lacked nothing. However, this was not enough for them, as they went and made alliances with nations against God's will, for provision and protection from their enemies, when God was their protector and provider. Not only that, as soon as God started blessing them, they soon turned to worshipping idols and other gods of other nations. God saw their behavior as not only an act of rebellion, unfaithfulness, and insult, but also prostitution. Israel was 'married' to God, but they went out to seek other 'lovers'.

What lovers have you gone in search of? Is it material things? Sexual partners? Worldly pleasures? Israel ascribed all they had- their prosperity and security- to the false gods they served and alliances they formed with pagan nations (nations that worshipped false gods)- and only returned unto God when they were in trouble or found life's burdens too much for them to carry. Are you seeking God only because of what He can give you?

If you're guilty of this, do not worry or think you are a bad person; we are all guilty of this. However, I urge you to change your focus and instead of being religious, start pursuing God with all your heart so that you may know Him and worship Him as God. Everyone can praise God, but only those who love and develop a heart for God can truly worship Him IN SPIRIT AND IN TRUTH- that's the worship God requires from us- one that comes from the heart (John 4:23-24).

Moving Forward

As you go through this day, ask yourself, 'Why am I here? Is it to live a life of abundance? Or am I here to develop an intimate relationship with God and to fulfill God's will for my life?' God wants us to live an abundant life, but He does not want us to live it outside of Him. He wants to be a part of our everyday life and decisions, not only when we need something or life's throwing afflictions and hardship on us. Therefore, I urge you not to set your heart upon the things of this world, but upon the things that are of God. In due season God will bless you with material things and all the things you desire, as it is His will to bless you (Colossians 3:1-2; Matthew 6:31-33).

Day 41
There Is Power in Your Mouth

"Our God is a speaking God; when He wanted to do something, He spoke the words. Therefore, whatever we need, and when tempests arise and rock our boat, do not be fearful or worry; just SPEAK THE WORD!!"

Scriptures of the Day: Genesis 1: 26-28; Joshua 10:12-13; James 3: 6

Discourse

I strongly believe that over 70% of us as a people do not know who we are, and the power and authority God has given us. Let's look at who we are through God. God is our creator; when He was creating the universe, whatever He wanted He spoke the word, and what He said came to pass. The spoken words formed flesh. When Jesus told Peter to come out of the boat and walk on water, Peter did not walk on his own power, but he walked on the spoken word of God. The Bible said we are created in the image and likeness of God; therefore, we, too, have creative power within us. Since God is a speaking God, He created others that are like Him, but at the same time limited in ability.

When Jesus came to earth, he demonstrated the power that God gave to mankind when whatever he spoke came to pass. When Lazarus was dead, he called Lazarus to come alive and Lazarus walked out of the tomb alive (John 11:43-44). When the storm rocked the boat he and his disciples were in, he got up and rebuked the wind and the wind stopped (Mark 4:39). All that Jesus did while on earth was a manifestation of the awesome ability God had invested in them that understand the power God has given them and are willing to seek His face daily.

Many times the enemy backs us in a corner, and we look at our situation and think that this is it now; we will never be set free. Did you know that your current situation is not an indicator of what your tomorrow will be? Did you know that the position you may be in now, God has allowed it so that He may use it to bring out the creative power within you?

Too many times we allow the enemy to shut our mouths, and thus we continue day after day, month after month in the same condition. Aren't you by now tired of waking up with the same problems day after day? If you are, then its time you start speaking to your situation.

Words are one of the most powerful gifts God has given to every individual. The words you speak, they are not just mere words, but they have power; they are life. Just how powerful are our words? Words are the only thing that can transcend time, affecting the past, present and future, are not bound by geographical location, can affect our mood, feelings and perception without us even realizing, and can affect both the physical and the realm of the spirit at the same time. Words are so powerful that your mother could have spoken a word over your life fifty (50) years ago, and that word is still affecting your life either negatively or positively today. Words are not bound by where you live or any geographical location. That is why the Bible says in Proverbs 18:21 that "Death and life are in the power of the tongue: and they that love it shall eat the fruit thereof." Power is in your mouth to change the atmosphere around you and your life.

The Bible also declares that the tongue is the most deadly thing we have, "that it defileth the whole body, and setteth on fire the course of nature..." So that "Out of the same mouth proceedeth blessing and cursing" (James 3: 6, 11).

The words you speak can keep you in poverty all the days of your life, can bring healing to your mind and body, and can deliver you out of any situation the enemy may throw in your face.

Moving Forward

As you go through this day, use your mouth to affect your day and any situation you may encounter. If you say with confidence you will have a very miserable day, then you will have a very miserable day. The atmosphere is affected by your words- because you have creative power. Use your mouth to always speak positive, to bless and not to curse, to build up and not to destroy. God has entrusted you with the spoken word; use it for good and not evil. Whatever situations you may find yourself in, speak life. For example: do not say your sickness will never get better, but say with confidence, 'I will get better.' Whenever anyone speaks negative words over your life or children or someone you love, you have the power to reverse those curse words.

Day 42

Can God Trust You?

Can God trust you when it seems as if He is not there? When you are away from those who know that you are a child of God, can He trust you to remain faithful to Him? Can God trust you when everyone around is serving another God other than the true and living God?

Scriptures of the Day: Daniel 1:8-14; 3: 8-18

Discourse

We read the story in the Bible of Daniel and the three Hebrew boys, Shadrach, Meshach and Abednego, who stood for God even when they were living in a foreign land where sin was very prominent. Daniel and his three friends, along with most of the people of Judea, were taken to Babylon by King Nebuchadnezzar when Judea rejected God. Despite being in a sinful environment and God's people following the custom of the land, these four men did not allow the influence of the people around them to lead them into a sinful life.

Can God trust you enough to send you to university away from your family, friends and church brethren, and know that despite the school environment, you will not exchange your salvation for the pleasures of this world? Can God put you in a very sinful environment and know that you will not defile your temple with the sinful conversation and conduct of those you will come in contact with? Will you stand for God even though no one else is standing, or will you follow the crowd?

God is looking for people that know who they are, and will refuse to exchange Him for the god of money, sex, material things, and other pleasures of this world. Each day we face numerous temptations, whether it may be at the workplace, school environment, walking on the road, through the media, and even in the House of God. The enemy knows our weakness and will use it to destroy us. Our flesh is one of our biggest hindrances to us living a holy life. That is why whenever you turn on the television or walk on the street you are bombarded with images of beauty, sex, money and other worldly pleasures, so as to condition your mind to desire the things that God hates; it is a war against good and evil, God and Satan. It is a war to see who will have your soul. The decision of who will win the battle for your soul is totally in your hands; God or Satan, who will it be?

Those who have made up in their mind to serve God must do like Daniel and the three Hebrew boys; they must resist sin with every ounce of strength they have. Every generation from the beginning of time had their own battles to fight; none is more difficult than the other. The only thing that has changed is the method and the scale on which the battle is being fought, but each person in each generation had their own struggles. Daniel, Shadrach, Meshach and Abednego were no different than us. They too had struggles, were tempted to sin, had peer pressure all around them, had numerous opportunities to sin and then repent as we all do at times, were bombarded with images of sex, the choice of going to the hottest party, and faced oppositions for standing up for God; but despite the many odds that were against them and the intensity of the battles they had to fight each day, they decided in their minds that they would serve God. They would not sell out their salvation for parties, sex, education, and worldly pleasures. They knew that even though they were in a strange land and God had turned His back on them, He was still watching them and was still in control. They knew that serving God would not be easy, but they knew that if they stood up for God and did not bow to the idols of the land, then God would stand with them and deliver them out of all their troubles.

Moving Forward

Daniel and his friends taught us that no matter where we are, or at what stage we're at in our life, if we avail ourselves to God, then He can elevate and use us to do great things. God will exalt you in the midst of your friends and enemies; you don't have to follow the behaviors and customs of the world to enjoy life and to be someone with great influence. As you go through this day, there will be opportunities to do the things that are not of God, and you will be tempted to sin against God, but I encourage you to be like Daniel and the three Hebrew boys; let God trust you with temptations.

Part 6

Ministry/Purpose

"When you are called for ministry and doing the will of God, there will be times when you will feel like you will not make it and you cry out to The Lord, "Lord, save us: we perish,' because of the attacks of the enemy. When you are called to do a work, no weapon that is formed against you shall prosper, because the work of the Lord must be done."

Scriptures of the Day: Mark 4:35-41; Isaiah 54: 15-17

Discourse

There was a time when Jesus said unto his disciples; come let us go over to the other side of the lake, because there was work to be done. So they went into a boat, but while they were going across the water, leaving from one side to the other, a contrary wind rose up trying to stop them. The Bible says, "And, behold, there arose a great tempest in the sea, insomuch that the ship was covered with the waves: but he was asleep" (Matthew 8:24).

There are three 'problems' in this story:

1. Jesus called his disciples to accompany him to the other side, for there was a work to be done, however, in the midst of going over to the other side there arose a great tempest so much that the disciples saw death before them; they became fearful as they thought they were going to die.

2. The disciples were struggling to stay alive and Jesus is in the boat, sleeping, comfortable, while they are about to die. Perhaps facing their last moments on earth, they started thinking about their family back home; they didn't get to say goodbye and express their love. They were young and there were still things they wanted to do with their lives; facing death makes you start thinking of what you could do, or should have done better with your life. The disciples perhaps were facing the

most dangerous period of not only their life, but their walk with Jesus. They perhaps were greatly anticipating the day they would start doing some of the miracles they saw Jesus do, in hopes of seeing the physical manifestation of the kingdom of God on earth, but death was knocking at their door, and Jesus was right there in the boat, not trying to help, but sleeping.

3. The third issue with this scenario is that they awoke Jesus and let him know of their dilemma and Jesus turned to them and chastised them. "Why are ye fearful, O ye of little faith?"- Mark 4:40. What? Did Jesus just chastise them for being concerned about their lives? Didn't Jesus see that the wind was very heavy and the sea raging mightily, and the worst part, they were not on land but in the water? Perhaps they would have had a better chance of surviving on land, but not so much in the water fighting against the elements of nature. Jesus chastises them for being fearful.

But why did Jesus chastise his disciples for being fearful? What did Jesus want his disciples to understand? Surely he saw their predicament.

When we are called for ministry or to do the work of the Lord, Jesus sometimes will say to us, come, "Let us go over unto the other side of the lake" (Luke 8:22), and while we are joyfully going about the work of the Lord we face situations that are contrary to the word of the Lord. For example, 'Go preach the gospel in your community and many souls will be saved'- nothing is said about oppositions you will face or any near death experience. Jesus and his disciples were on their way to deliver a man possessed with demons, and people were also there to hear the word of the Lord; the enemy, therefore, knowing that Jesus was coming, sought to stop him on his way. This was not a mere storm, but it was a massive attack by Principalities (Prince demons that control territories or regions) who knew that if they should allow Jesus to land on their territory, he could cause trouble for them. Once we are called by God, the enemy knows it and will send out weapons of mass destruction to stop us. People that know their purpose and what they are about are a dangerous treat to the enemy.

Isn't it strange how sometimes the Lord can send us to do His work, but is in our boat taking a nap? What did Jesus want his disciples to understand about why he chastised them?

Jesus wanted his disciples and us today to know that:

1. Whenever he sends you on a mission, he will show you the end- that you will go to the other side- but he will at times not show you the storm between where you are coming from, and where he is taking you. Despite this, do not be fearful because if he says you're going to the other side, no Prince demons, witches, warlocks or agents of Satan will be able to stop you. Even if you get thrown overboard into the raging sea you shall not die, because no weapons that form against you shall be able to prosper; it is your inheritance. When the enemy attacks you, the Lord wants you to open your mouth and remind him of who you are and that no weapon that forms against you shall be able to prosper.

2. He wanted the disciples and us today to understand that even if it seems like Jesus is in our boat sleeping, he will never allow the enemy to destroy them. The weapon may form- the wind was blowing heavily and the water was raging- but the intent of the weapon will not come to pass- the enemy wanted to destroy them in the water, but Jesus stepped in and rebuked the wind and everything went calm.

3. He wanted to increase their faith. Many times the Lord will allow the enemy to attack us in certain areas of our lives and or ministry because he wants to increase our faith in him, and for us to know who we are and what we possess. The Lord cannot teach you warfare without allowing you to be attacked by the enemy, as how will you fight when legions are coming at you? If He doesn't start training you to pray effectively, how will you pray when you are called upon to pray at a big event? How will you know how to use your authority and gifts if He does not put you in the fire? In the natural, before a company starts giving you certain responsibilities they first have to train or see how you handle certain responsibilities- as it is in the physical, so it is in the

spiritual.

Moving Forward

As you go through this day and face the rest of your life, remember God will never send you throughout life and ministry without first knowing how He will deliver you out of every situation. Do not be fearful when things are happening contrary to what He says, as God has everything under control and He is trying to teach you something. Nothing that happens, or will happen to you, whether in your ministry, job, family or health, is bigger than your God. Yes, at times you may feel fearful as you are human, but remember His promise that He will never leave you nor forsake you until the end of the world.

Day 44
Don't Let that Dream or Purpose Die

"It is the plan of the enemy to discourage and frustrate the people of God so that they will stop doing the work/will of the Lord. For years the enemies of Judea frustrated and tried to hinder them from rebuilding the Temple, but they continued in the midst of deadly opposition. You might feel discouraged now and feel like throwing in the towel, but God is with you and will finish the work He started. Like the Jews, you shall have your shout at the end if you faint not."

Scriptures of the Day: Nehemiah 4: 1-3, 4-5; 1 Kings 19

Discourse

How many times have you felt like throwing in the towel and said, whether outwardly or by your action, 'Lord, this is it, I am finished. Life it is too much for me to handle. Lord, what you call me to do is too much. I cannot continue doing your work anymore. I will not carry these heavy burdens anymore. Lord, I am finished with you and life.'

If you reach this point in your life and or ministry, then it means you're being attacked by the enemy. It means that the enemy sees something in you and he is trying to bring you to the abortion table for you to abort that gift, ministry or that purpose that is growing inside of you. It means you are stepping into another dimension or level in your life and the enemy doesn't like it, so he will use everything he can to stop you.

If you're in this position, then you need to stop right now and shout, because God is about to do something exciting in your job, ministry and or life.

Whenever God is about to do something in a person's life or upon the earth, the enemy will always send his assassins to stop it. Who are his assassins? Persecution, problems on the job all of a sudden, your boss and co-workers giving you trouble, trouble in your marriage and family life, financial turmoil, health issues, your friends turned against you, demonic attacks on a whole different level, and the list goes on. The enemy will use anything he can to stop you. When Jesus came to this earth, Herod tried to destroy the promise seed. When the Jews were rebuilding their temple in Jerusalem, the enemy rose up powerful oppositions to stop the move of God.

Whenever you find yourself in a tight situation and the enemy is attacking you at every level, do not complain, give in to the pressure of life and run, but start praising God for what He is about to do. You do not see the deliverance as yet, but praise Him in advance. When you praise and worship God despite what you're going through, you confuse the enemy because he cannot understand how he is doing so much to destroy you, but you still have a praise, you're still going into the house of God, you're still going to work and not holding any malice, grudge or bitterness against anyone.

Moving Forward

As you go through this day and you face the rest of your life, remember that troubles will come, but God is faithful. I have proven the awesome power of praise and worship, as many times I am sick, and all I did was worship and in a few minutes, sometimes seconds, all pains are gone. Healing and deliverance is our inheritance. Joy, peace and happiness is our inheritance. God wants you to praise Him despite of what you're going through, and the more you praise Him, the more confused the enemy will be and the faster your deliverance will come. It is the job of the enemy to stop you from doing the work of the Lord, to live an empowered life or to manifest your purpose, but it is your duty to fight him with all you have and not to throw in the towel.

I can't wait to see you tomorrow. Have a blessed and fulfilling day...

Don't abort your purpose.

Day 45
Follow Your Dream or Vision

"All God wants is one person to catch on to His vision of what He wants to do, and when that person does, He will empower that person to carry out His divine purpose- but expect opposition."

Scriptures of the Day: Nehemiah 4:1-23; Jeremiah 1: 17-19

Discourse

The children of Judah were sent into captivity in Babylon because of their sins against God. As a result of the siege against Jerusalem, the temple of God where God said He will put His name forever was destroyed because the people used the temple as an excuse to continue to sin against God. To this, the book of Jeremiah 7: 3 says, "This is what the Lord Almighty, the God of Israel, says: Reform your ways and your actions, and I will let you live in this place. Do not trust in deceptive words and say, "This is the temple of the Lord, the temple of the Lord, the temple of the Lord!" They therefore lived a life contrary to the word of God, because they thought that God would never destroy Jerusalem because of His temple.

There came a time when God wanted the temple to be rebuilt and Nehemiah answered the call. I want you to understand that if God is going to do something upon the earth, then He will find and prepare a man for the job. God will not always use a crowd to carry out his plan; all he needs is one man to say, 'Yes Lord, I am available to you.' Could you be that one man/woman the Lord is waiting on to carry out a special job? We read in the book of Nehemiah that he set out to do what God laid upon his heart to do, to rebuild the temple. However, this was not an easy task for him; not because he did not have the right team to work with him, or because he did not have the skills or resources to carry out the rebuilding of the temple; it was not an easy task because he met much opposition from powerful and influential people, and even from his own countrymen, but despite this he relied on God and His wisdom to survive (Nehemiah 4:1-3; 6:2-3,17-19). He stood up for the principles of God even when it seemed unfavorable for him to do so. He was ridiculed and they conspired to destroy him, but he stood his ground because he understood that God called him to do a job, and if God called him to do a job, then God will send the right people to help him, and give him the wisdom and strength to carry out His work.

What is God laying on your heart to do? What do you see that needs to be done? What is your ministry that you are afraid of manifesting? Perhaps you are afraid of oppositions or you believe you are not the right person for the job. God did not call any of us to be spectators in life, but He called us to use what talents or gifts He gave us to fulfill a need.

The story of Nehemiah teaches us that not only will God find and prepare a man to do something, but He will use that person to inspire and or train others to accomplish what He called that man to do. When God calls you for a task, he will strengthen and give you all you need to accomplish His work, including the right people. If you say God called you to do something, and He hasn't given you the skills and or tools to do it and the right people around you to complete the task, then you need to go back and do a recheck to see who called you. He will not give you all you need all at once; but He will not give you a job to do and not equip you.

What tool has God put in your hand to do His work? Approximately ninety percent (90%) of this book, and some of the articles on my site (biblewaymag.com), were written totally from my mobile phone. What if I had said, 'Lord, you told me to write this book, but I don't have any computer or laptop to do so." Stop wasting time complaining of what you have or don't have; when God called you, He knew all you have and don't have. The God we serve is not an unkind boss who will put you to work without equipping you with something to start the work. I am not saying you should not ask, but while you are asking and waiting patiently, use what you have until He blesses you with what you need.

When God gave Moses the plan to build the ark of the Covenant, God had already spent years training and preparing supports for the job; all Moses did was give instructions and others who had the skill did what the man of God envisioned through God to do (Exodus 31:1-6).

We further learnt from Nehemiah that when you are chosen for a task there will be opposition that will try to stop the work. We saw that when Sanballat heard of the rebuilding of the wall, he ridiculed the Jews in the presence of his friends (Nehemiah 4:1-3). By ridiculing the work of the Lord, they were hoping that Nehemiah and the Jews would become discouraged and afraid and the work would have stopped. What did Nehemiah do when he heard their insults? He prayed unto God and encouraged himself in the Lord, and the people worked with all their hearts (vs 4-8).

We further learnt that when their enemies learnt that the work continued, they started plotting to destroy the Jews. This is when Nehemiah started using his leadership skills and set men as guards (vs 8-9); not only that, Nehemiah was willing to listen to who was around him. You must understand that just because you were the one God gave the vision to do the work, it doesn't mean you will know and see everything. No one man is an island; a bird cannot fly with one wing.

Moving Forward

Jesus said unto his disciples, "The harvest is plentiful but the workers are few. Ask the Lord of the harvest, therefore, to send out workers into his harvest field" (Matthew 9:37-38); are you willing to go out and do the work of the Lord? Are you willing to follow your dream or vision so that you can live an empowered life? All the Lord needs is one person to use as a vessel, and then others will follow. Opposition(s) will come, but the Lord will give you the strength to carry out His task. The amazing thing about standing up against opposition is that those who opposed, at the end, will repent and join you.

Day 46
Do Not Neglect the Gift

"Each one of us has been given gift(s) that will make our names great if we use it effectively. Your gift could be your voice, you're a great writer, your musical skills, leadership skills, etc., or it could be some spiritual gifts; for example, the gift of prophesy. The gift is not to be neglected, nor is it for you; but your gift is for the building/edification of someone else."

Scriptures of the Day: 1 Corinthians 12:1- 11, 27-31; Proverbs 18:16

Discourse

When you look at some of the prominent characters in the Bible, for example, Joseph, and Moses, one thing you will readily notice is that each of them were gifted differently, but at the same time could not have completed the task God gave them if they did not use their gift(s) or talents.

All of us were put on this earth for a purpose, and to fulfill that purpose God has invested skills and gifts in each one of us to carry out our purpose, and to live a meaningful and bountiful life. The Bible says, "A gift opens the way and ushers the giver into the presence of the great" (Proverbs 18:16, NIV). Each one of us has the potential to be great and do exceptional things; that's why God has invested gifts in each one of us. The gift(s) you are carrying right now is powerful enough to bring you before thousands of people and before great men and women. You may say, my gift is to bake cakes and that cannot make my name great; but did you know that you could develop a recipe that's on the lips of millions of people around the globe? Or you could start a world famous cooking show or blog that is watched and or read by millions around the world. Never look at what God has given you and say you cannot use it to do great things, and never look at yourself and say you cannot be great. Greatness is within you! Martin Luther King or Oprah Winfrey did not become world famous personalities by looking at what others could contribute to society; no, they looked at what they could contribute to society by using their gifts and talents.

Let me ask you a question: why should you live your life unfulfilled when God has blessed you with the tools to fulfill your life from conception? You are unhappy not because you are not blessed, but because you chose to be unhappy. Happiness is what you make it; whether you have plenty or not, one leg or hand or both, you can be happy if you choose. If you are not doing great things right now, are poor and or living a miserable life, it is not because God did not give you what it takes to be great or exceptional. Exceptionality and greatness is in the palm of your hand; you can choose to let it go, or to hold unto it and use it.

Many of you reading this book right now, God is about to usher you into your purpose and is about to make your name great. However, you will not be great if you do not acknowledge and walk in your time or season. Many times we do not walk in our destiny because we do not realize our destiny when it comes knocking; therefore, we let the opportunity God has given us pass us by, and then we murmur or complain that God does not love us. Or, we sit every day complaining that we are broke, when God opened the door yesterday but you failed to walk through it. When God opens a door, it is your duty to make every effort to walk through that open door.

Sometimes the Lord will have you in a position, job or family situation for years, and you consistently question the Lord and ask the Lord to take you out of that situation, but He remains silent to your pleas. I want you to understand that everything and every experience you have been through are for a reason. Joseph could not understand why his brothers sold him into Egypt as a slave when the Lord gave him such remarkable dreams, and why he had to go to prison for many years. Like many of us, he probably questioned God about his situation and probably for a short moment hated his brothers for what they did. However, God was grooming him for his ultimate purpose, one that he could not see or understand at the time. In Potiphar house, Joseph was Chief Stewart and Scribe (according to history) for Potiphar, and so was put in charge of all of his master's agricultural assets and household skills that he would need as Governor of Egypt. If Joseph did not go into the pit, then he would not have been elevated to one of the highest positions in Egypt and saved the known world from starvation, including his own family. What am I saying to you? I am trying to tell you that the pit is what will equip you with the necessary skills/talents/gifts that will make your name great.

Moses was able to use his leadership skills gained from living as a Prince in Egypt, and as a shepherd while in Midian, to lead God's people in the wilderness for over 40 years. Furthermore, he learnt humility, patience, perseverance and developed a relationship with God when he was sent to take care of sheep at the back of the mountains for 40 years. His experiences led him to be one of the greatest men ever to walk this earth; his gifts made room for him. The same can be said of great men and women of our time; for example, TD Jakes, Joel Osteen, Martin Luther King, and Bob Marley, among others.

Moving Forward

As you go through this day, take a moment to think about what gift or gifts you may be carrying. Are you using what God has given you? Someone is out there right now depending on you to be the next Martin Luther King, Louise Bennett, Moses, Joseph, Elisha, the next TD Jakes or Steve Jobs. Perhaps you have not been embracing it as you should and you desire something else. All of us have our individual part to play in society; all of us cannot be a doctor, pilot, prophet, or apostle, but all of us can be who God calls us to be.

Day 47
Do Not Let the Words of Others Stop You

"As people of God, let us not allow the mouths of others around us to hinder us from moving forward in God or to cause us to become spiritually paralyzed. One thing is certain, and that is people will always talk, so prepare for it and embrace it. If you faint not, you will come out as pure gold."

Scriptures of the Day: Matthew 12: 22-30; Mark 3: 21-22; John 15:18-21

Discourse

One of the things that Jesus faced in his three and half years of ministry that was constant throughout, was that people spoke negative words about him, even in his presence. In one of Jesus' 'talk' with his chosen disciples that should continue his work, he encouraged them not to faint when they were ridiculed and persecuted (Matthew 10: 24-25).

Everything Jesus said and all that happened to him is a lesson for us today. One lesson is that people will always talk- when we do well, they will talk, and when we make a mistake, they will crucify us. That is a fact of life. Since this is a constant fact of life, are you going to allow the words of people to hinder you from fulfilling your purpose? Are you going to allow the words of your co-workers to make you not want to go to work each day or do your job the right way? Are you going to allow the mouths of a few people who have no other purpose but to talk push you out of church, or have sleepless nights while they are sleeping comfortably?

There was a time when Jesus was casting demons out of a young man and instead of rejoicing, the Pharisees out of jealousy started accusing Jesus of casting out demons through the power of Beelzebub. If they called Jesus Beelzebub, what will they not call you (Matthew 10:24-25)? Jesus did not allow their hurtful insults to hinder or stop him from fulfilling his purpose; nor did he hate or hold any grudge against them. When the enemy sees that you are a threat to his kingdom, he will use words to distract or stop you.

If you will become anything in life and will have a great ministry, there is a cost to pay. This is a fact of life that you cannot escape regardless of what field you're in, where you are at in your career or what ministry you serve in the Kingdom of God.

Many of us allow the words of others to hinder us from moving forward in God and in life. When you allow this to happen, they are not the ones being affected or not fulfilling their purpose- you are! You are the one that will live your life unfulfilled and will be judged for not using your talents to the glory of God. God was the one who died for you, so He is the only one that should dictate to you how you should think, believe or live your life. No one has the right to stop you from fulfilling your purpose, and when you allow their words to stop you from doing so, then you are giving them power over your life that they should not have in the first place.

Yes, words hurt, but you will have to wipe your tears, forgive them and move on. Jesus died so that you may live an empowered life, a life of victory.

Moving Forward

As you go through this day and face the rest of your life, let us forget those negative words that have been spoken against us and move on to higher levels in God, our career, our family and in life overall. People will talk; that's their job. Your job is to objectively analyze what's being said (as sometimes they have some valid criticisms), take out the junk and apply what needs to be applied to your life while holding no grudge against anyone. If there is no opposition in a race, then the crown at the end will be meaningless.

"For do I (Paul) now persuade men, or God? or do I seek to please men? for if I yet pleased men, I should not be the servant of Christ" (Galatians 1:10).

Day 48
Anointed to Serve

"Like Esther was placed in the kingdom to be a deliverer to his people, likewise each one of us was placed in the kingdom for such a time as this. Do not worry about those that come to hinder or stop you from accomplishing your purpose, because like Haman, the same weapon that is used against you will be used to destroy your enemies. Also, the Lord will use your enemies to be the catalyst to your blessings. You were born to give the devil hell."

Scriptures of the Day: Esther 4: 10-17; 6:1-11

Discourse

I want each one of you reading this book to take a moment to think about what your purpose for being alive right now is. Why did God create you? Surely it was not just to have a fancy car, a beautiful house, to raise beautiful children, to only go to church every Saturday or Sunday. What is your purpose?

The fact is, each one of us was put on this earth for a divine purpose, to fulfill a need. My purpose is to deliver and elevate God's people through teaching, preaching, books, and the working of my gifts; at least, that's what is being revealed to me at this moment. Your purpose might be different; perhaps your purpose is to be a teacher, a prophet, or a pastor, the CEO of company, or the next leader of your country; perhaps your purpose is to be a deliverance minister or a Counselor. Your purpose may be one, or two, or many. The truth is, when we were born and when we came into the kingdom, God gave each one of us gift(s), skills or talents that will help us to fulfill our purpose in life or in ministry. Each one of us has a ministry and/or a purpose in life; it may not be an evangelist or some officer in the church, but you have a ministry; or your purpose may not even be in the church.

Another fact is, when God called you into his glorious kingdom, he had to open a door for you to go through. In other words, all of us are called to fulfill a specific need or needs, and someone is depending on what each one of us has. I am depending on my religious leader to be my spiritual shepherd, and so my spiritual growth may be hindered if he fails to perform his duties. I am depending on my doctor to give me the right diagnoses of any health issues I may have. What need am I, or someone in your generation, depending on you to fulfill?

You may be thinking right now that your life does not have a purpose; but that is a deceptive lie from the devil. No one would have created a computer if there wasn't a need for it; likewise, God would not have created you if you did not serve a purpose. Your life has meaning!

We were made a miracle to be someone else's miracle. Whose miracle are you carrying? Who is out there waiting for you to start walking in your divine calling? The day I decide I will no longer do the work of the Lord or walk in my purpose could be the day someone commits suicide because I failed to do what I was called to do. If all the police officers decide they are going to stay home from work, that could be the day you lose your life by the hands of gunmen.

Moving Forward

As you go through this day, please take a moment to think about why you are here. If you do not know your purpose, then it's time you start seeking God in prayer and maybe fasting until He answers. Whatever God has given you, He will be judging you based on what you do with His gift(s). Let each one of us not be like the man who took his one talent and buried it. Can you imagine what would happen if all the doctors in your country should strike tomorrow? Do not deprive someone else of what you have. You are called to serve, not yourself, but others, as it's not about you or how you may feel.

Day 49
Broken, But in All the Right Places

"Like Moses driven from Egypt into the desert, broken and beaten, likewise the Lord breaks us until we are fit for the master's use. Like Moses taken from royalty to as low as tending to sheep so he could humble and train him for His purpose, likewise the Lord humbles and trains us for His purpose."

Scripture of the Day: Exodus 2

Discourse

We cannot always fathom the mind of God or understand why He does things the way He does at times. When I was growing up I hated the story of Moses and would never watch the movie, because I could not understand why God had to take Moses from royalty so that he could deliver his people. My thought at the time was, why didn't God elevate Moses to the position of Pharaoh and then have him set his people free? Surely he didn't have to make Moses run for his life. I was, at the time, looking at it through my own subjective views and not trying to see things from God's point of view.

That is a problem we all face at times, seeing things through our own subjective lenses. God does not always think like we do, nor does He promise that He will subject Himself to our thinking or that He will show us the full purpose of why He is taking us into a certain direction while we are in the process. Moses did not know that God was humbling him and teaching him how to lead his people as a shepherd leads its sheep when he had him taking care of sheep. God made him into a prince of Egypt and then stripped him of every essence of royalty and authority so He could train him to lead his rebellious people for 40 years in the wilderness, like a shepherd leads his sheep to green pastures.

Everything Moses needed to be who God wanted him to be- leadership skills, patience, humility, love, the heart of God, gentleness, and a warrior- God gave it unto Moses while he was in Pharaoh's palace, traveling in the wilderness to Midian, and during the 40 years he spent tending to his father-in-law's sheep, to carry out God's redemptive plan.

The Lord will give you a high paying job, a nice house, car, money and other material things, and then suddenly take it away from you. Nothing you have in life is forever, and sometimes why the Lord blesses you a certain way or puts you in certain position is because He wants to teach you something; if he chooses, He can remove you when He sees fit. That is why some people had to come out of your life, you had to be broken, you had to lose everything you had, you had to go into the hospital struggling to survive, you had to lose some valuable things; He did it because He wants to nurture you for a divine purpose. That is why when the Lord takes some things from you or allows the enemy to strip you as he did with Job, you should not become hostile, angry or depressed: because He is teaching you something and bringing you into your purpose, or he is using what you go through to help or deliver someone in similar or worse situation(s). Moses' purpose was not to be a prince or king in Egypt; he was handpicked and groomed to be the deliverer of God's people, but God could not just elevate him to such a position, as he would not have the necessary skills to handle the task.

God was the one who was ordering Moses' life; sometimes we think we are the author and finisher of our own life, but the reason why you have your job, you went to college, you got married, etc., is because God is directing your life in the direction He wants you to take. Yes, sometimes we will stray from the direction God is leading us, but He will always find a way to bring us back in line.

Moving Forward

You may be broken, but in the right place; broken, but not according to the will of the devil, but according to the will of God. The enemy thought he had Moses under his control, but what he didn't know was that God was preparing Moses for a major purpose. Will you have a good attitude even when you don't understand what the Lord is doing in your life? As you go through this day, remember that at times the Lord will put you in the wilderness so that He may train you for a divine purpose.

Day 50
Wrestling with God for Your Breakthrough

"Like Jacob wrestled with God and would not let him go until He blessed him; like Esther said if I perish, I perish, but I must see the king; so does the Lord want us to seek after Him with great zeal."

Scriptures of the Day: Job 23: 8-15; Esther 4: 10-17

Discourse

David knew what it meant to be determined and or desperate for God when he said in Psalms 42:1, "As the hart panteth after the water brooks, so panteth my soul after thee, O God." When the hart is out hunting and is parched with thirst and in the burning heat of the sun, he will seek desperately after water as if his life was depending on it, desperate for just a little water from the brook, and when the hart reaches to the water brooks he will plunge in as if he had been seeking water for days and was just about to die from thirst.

There will be times in our lives when the Lord will take us to a point where we feel like he is not there; we feel alone and empty and as if something special is missing from our lives. Like David, we search for him desperately just to feel a touch from Him. It is at these times in our lives the Lord is desiring us to come up to another level. Similarly, many times when God wants us to come up higher He will take away some things from us so that we will seek after Him with great desperation, like the hart goes after the water because his life depends on it for survival. The Bible tell us that Job was in a similar situation when he searched diligently for God but could not find him anywhere; however, he knew that when God hath tried him, he would come out as pure gold as the Lord held his steps (Job 23: 8-15).

God does not want us to merely live our lives as individuals, but He wants us to wrestle with Him through constant prayers, regular fasting, worship and praise, studying the Bible, and concerning ourselves with the things of God. Many times we fail to understand that why the Lord sometimes allows persecution and different issues to come into our lives is because He wants to take us to another dimension.

Esther could have lost her life for going to see the king without being summoned, but she made up in her mind that she will not stand by and see her people destroyed. Seeking after God and doing His work may cost you a few friends, many sleepless nights, persecution, being lied about, mistreated by people around you, many days of not knowing where the next meal will come from, and humiliation, among other things. However, the reward of knowing that you taught or preached a message or lesson and someone learnt something from it, you laid your hands and people being healed, your life inspired and strengthened the faith of others, divine favor was over your life, and God used you to do many wonderful things, adequately compensates for all the troubles you will encounter seeking after and doing His will.

Jacob was determined that he would not let go of God until the Lord blessed him, even though it could have cost him his life. How far are you willing to go for God to take you to another level?

Moving Forward

As you go through this day and go through life, make up your mind that no matter what life may throw at you, you will seek after God with all your heart and might, because at the end of the day only what you do for God and your relationship with Him will matter- not the cars, having a beautiful house, having a high paying job, being in a happy marriage- all that is good, but at the end of the day only what you do for God and your relationship with Him truly matters- that's the whole purpose of you being born in the first place.

Day 51

Uncover the Roof with Your Faith

"Things will come in our lives to knock us off our feet, but we must decide to get back up. Moreover, there will be times the way to our breakthrough or purpose is all blocked off and there seems to be no way for us to reach where we want to go to be delivered, or to accomplish our goals; but we must be determined to be like the man with the palsy, and uncover the roof with your faith."

Scripture of the Day: Mark 2: 1-12

Discourse

For our final devotional message, I want us to go off with a bang by looking at the man in the Bible that was sick with the palsy. There was a time when Jesus in his ministry went into a house while in Capernaum and, like always, many people came to him to be delivered and to hear what he had to teach them.

Now what was so significant about this occasion was that four men brought a man that was sick with the palsy to see Jesus. These men could not get into the house because of the crowd. Now the logical thing to do on this occasion was to go home, but these men decided they were going to see Jesus no matter what it may cost. What these men decided to do was to climb upon the roof, with the man on his bed, remove the roof and let the man down to Jesus. The man, sick with the palsy, was made whole because these four men chose to do the most illogical thing. Their action showed their faith in Jesus, that if they could just bring him before Jesus then the man with the palsy would be made whole.

You may not be sick with the palsy, but you may face other life challenges that hold you down physically, emotionally, psychologically and/or spiritually for days, months, and even years. Like the woman with the issue of blood, you tried everything that you could think of, doctors, friends, drugs, alcohol, the opposite sex amongst others, but the situation(s) remained the same.

You may have become depressed, oppressed and felt like you wanted to give up on life by committing suicide or doing some other crazy stuff, but let me ask you one question: how strong is your faith in God? The Bible said if we have faith like a mustard seed, we can move mountains. What is the mountain in your life? Your mountain could be sex, drugs, some other form of addiction, lust, pornography, social media, illness, stuck in a broken relationship, not able to advance in your career and life, and the list goes on; there is no problem or mountain that is too big that God cannot make flat. God said in the book of Zechariah 4:7, "Who art thou, O great mountain? Thou shalt become plain..."

It is God's will that you be delivered and set free from sickness, homosexuality, addiction and everything that holds you captive. However, for God to work in your life you have to take the first step. The men saw the crowd but did not let the obstacle that was before them stop them. Whenever we are trying to go forward, there will always be some obstacles trying to stop us; however, every obstacle can be removed.

What is the Goliath or Great Mountain in your life? If you just have a little faith that God can use, then your faith will uncover the roof that is stopping you from receiving your blessings or stopping you from moving forward in your marriage, career, ministry and or education. It's not by your might or power that you will uncover the roof with your faith, but it is through the power of God.

Moving Forward

As you go through this day and your life lies before you, if someone should open the book of your life, what troubles would jump out at them from these pages? Perhaps the things of this world are suffocating the very life out of you and you feel like you're about to die; maybe like the man with palsy, you went to Jesus for help but the door was blocked by people or circumstances, and you are about to throw in the towel because you face problems on the job, spouse issues, a financial crisis, sickness rocking your body from the crown of your head to the soles of your feet, and you're thinking, 'This is it now, I'm done. I will never rise out of this state, so it's best I take my own life. It's better this way.' That's a lie from the pit of hell. Do not sit down and accept what the enemy or your situation is telling you. You shall arise from the ashes of despair and live again. God says LIFE, and not death. God says joy, peace, prosperity, happiness and abundant life, not a life of hopelessness, despair; not a life that feels and looks like a battlefield. God wants you to live again and live abundantly. Life throws you down, now it's time to get up with a bang. Thank you for joining me on this journey to An Empowered Life!

Author's Note

It was such a pleasure to write this book and I hope you enjoyed reading it and found it very helpful. An Empowered Life is my first book and it meant a lot that I could write this book to inspire and uplift you. Each day brings with it its own sets of troubles; I hope that you found An Empowered Life very helpful in understanding and overcoming some of the trials you face each day. When I started writing this book, I set out to write a book that would empower people to become who God called them to be. God did not create you to just merely exist, but he created you to positively change your environment.

The power is in our hands to bring about change in the world we live in, but first we must change how we think, speak, and act. If I can just change someone's perspective, or help one person to be more than what they are now, then I have accomplished what I had set out to do.

Like many of you, I was living a defeated life even after giving my life to Jesus, but one day I decided that enough was enough. I was not going to continue living my life like a weakling, feeling insignificant and not walking in my purpose; I decided that I was going to start being who God called me to be despite the oppositions, the negative perception and attitude of other. This is my life, and I will have to give an account to God for it.

Please let me know what you think of my book by leaving a review on Social Media sites, on your favorite online retailer and also on GoodReads. I would love to hear from you, so get in touch with me by visiting my personal site at http://www.estonswaby.com. You will also find new products by me. Visit http://www.biblewaymag.com for helpful articles. If you know someone that would find this book very helpful, please buy them a copy. Lastly, let your friends on social media know about An Empowered Life.

Whether you bought this book, or someone gave it to you as a gift, thank you for taking the time to read it. I hope that I was able to uplift, and inspire you to be the person God created you to be. You are uncontainable.......
Eston Swaby

Made in the USA
Columbia, SC
17 April 2022